Succession Planning:
Ensuring Smooth Transitions for Lawyers and their Firms

EDITED BY KATERINA MENHENNET

Commissioning editor
Katerina Menhennet

Managing director
Sian O'Neill

Succession Planning: Ensuring Smooth Transitions for Lawyers and their Firms
is published by

Globe Law and Business Ltd
3 Mylor Close
Horsell
Woking
Surrey GU21 4DD
United Kingdom
Tel: +44 20 3745 4770
www.globelawandbusiness.com

Succession Planning: Ensuring Smooth Transitions for Lawyers and their Firms

ISBN 9781787428393
EPUB ISBN 9781787428409
Adobe PDF ISBN 9781787428416

Contents

Executive summary

Partners are the lifeblood of law firms; they are responsible for bringing in business, implementing firm strategy, and leading their firm and clients through good times and bad. Therefore, the exit or loss of a partner can have a huge impact on a firm, yet only a small number have a succession plan in place. Coupled with this is the current succession crisis firms are facing, with law firm partnership, and ultimately leadership, becoming less attractive to junior lawyers, many of whom place greater importance on work–life balance than reaching top leadership levels. Consequently, creating a culture where client service and leadership is transitioned in a routine and organized fashion has never been more important, with the shift to remote working also enhancing the need to institutionalize such processes. A strong succession plan allows senior partners to retire with dignity, effective and well-prepared new leaders to step into their roles, the firm to maintain its fiscal health, and its clients and employees to continue to grow and flourish.

There are two essential elements of a successful succession plan within a law firm. The first is the transfer of clients from one generation to the next, and the second is the transition of firm management to a new generation. Both elements must take place in order for law firms to continue to prosper, and firms that develop and implement a succession plan are far more likely to achieve this. In our opening chapter, Sandra J. Boyer, founder and president of Legus International, discusses why the creation of a succession plan is important, how to create buy-in for its development, the components of a successful plan, how to implement it, and how to follow up to ensure consistent processes and procedures. With practical checklists outlining key points to remember, Sandra demonstrates how both management and client transitions can successfully be planned for and implemented, as well as providing warnings on possible obstacles and raising other issues that must be considered, including compensation and communication strategies.

Succession happens in all business enterprises, but particular attention must be given to the specificities of the legal profession and the character of law firms as service providers. Where individuals are strong their departure leaves a hole, and our second chapter by Hermann Knott, partner at KUNZ Lawyers, takes a closer look at the perspective of the senior lawyer on how they can best approach succession in order to mitigate this. After outlining the different types of succession that can occur in law firms, Hermann investigates the two most important factors when it comes to choosing the right option for your firm, timing and the size of the law firm, as well as how to manage the process. He examines the importance of early planning and considers the differences between succession in large and smaller law firms. The chapter concludes with a look at how firms can identify and develop their future leaders, and a suggestion that the succession process offers medium-sized and smaller firms in particular the opportunity to perform a strategic review of the future of their firm.

Our next chapter takes a look outside the firm towards its clients. The threat of losing clients, and thus revenue, as Baby Boomer partners continue to retire in large and disproportionate numbers is significant. The best approach to long-term stability in a client base is to inculcate succession planning into talent and client lifecycles, rather than treating it as a one-time event. Susan Saltonstall Duncan of RainMaking Oasis provides a framework for helping firms to achieve this. She begins by explaining why firms must follow a consistent approach to client transitions for all partners, and proceeds to outline the components of this approach, including discerning which clients are at risk, developing deeper and broader knowledge of each client, selecting the right successor, and developing, executing, and monitoring a transition plan for each partner and client. Susan also discusses the importance of active communication and engagement with clients during the transition, and concludes with a practical client transition checklist to aid firms in retaining clients over the long-term.

Firms must prepare for the succession of all partners, and those that contribute more towards reputation and turnover – the "rainmakers" – need particular attention. A small number might be responsible for a substantial part of revenue, reputation, and profitability, and they are also commonly the opinion leaders, which makes their successful succession especially crucial. However, there are inherent problems that result from the rainmaker status that contribute to challenges in planning for their succession. In chapter four, Jaap Bosman of TGO Consulting analyses and provides practical, hands-on advice on how to mitigate these problems. By outlining and discussing some of the key issues, including the ability of rainmakers to hold the firm hostage, their tendency to recruit weaker partners, and their reluctance to retire, Jaap demonstrates how firms can reduce tensions or remove them entirely, resulting in smooth rainmaker transitions.

Taking a step back from the debate about the lack of future partners and how firms are going to survive from one generation to the next, chapter five by August J. Aquila of AQUILA Global Advisors, LLC stresses that firms must not forget the value of their senior partners and argues that developing compensation plans to keep productive retiring and retired equity partners on board, retaining crucial intellectual capital, will make any firm stronger. August explains how retiring partners can be compensated in a way that encourages smooth client transitions and provides the most benefit for the partner and the firm, as well as the revenue generating, non-revenue generating, and outside the firm options for retired partners. With practical examples of how partners in various succession scenarios can be compensated, this chapter shows the myriad of benefits of retaining retiring and retired partners, and how to ensure a win-win situation for both the firm and the partner.

In chapter six, Pam Loch, managing director of Loch Associates Group, looks at the impact of diversity considerations in succession planning. With diversity and inclusion issues high on the business agenda, the proven advantages of a more diverse workforce, and the dramatic rise in demand for high quality staff, firms need to start thinking about how they can sustainably transform their business into a more diverse and inclusive workplace, or risk losing valuable talent to more inclusive competitors and being exposed to reputationally damaging discrimination claims. Pam explains how succession planning could be the answer to this. She shows that by selecting the right planning team, and ensuring diversity is considered at each stage of the succession planning process, diverse succession can become the default, providing the firm with manifold benefits. The chapter also discusses the issues law firms need to consider when scoping out their diversity agenda, highlights the pitfalls of getting it wrong, and offers some tips and tricks to successfully future-proof firms through succession planning in today's increasingly diversity-led culture.

Our next chapter focuses on some of the financial considerations involved in succession planning. Veronica Mann of Talis Financial Advisers outlines the key concerns the firm and the individual must consider to allow a succession plan to be financially successful. She begins by suggesting potential obstructions and hindrances to a succession plan and goes on to discuss a variety of elements that, if addressed effectively, will ensure a successful one. These include having clear partnership or director/shareholder agreements; financial planning for individuals to allow for a comfortable retirement, including advice on different potential income streams; measures to put in place to mitigate the consequences of the unexpected loss of key players; and the consideration of future liabilities. Through providing sound financial advice, Veronica demonstrates how firms and individuals can ensure smooth successions from this standpoint.

Next up is a deep dive into a specialist succession scenario – that of when a sole practitioner comes to sell their practice. With new technologies making it easier than ever to set up a law firm, sole practitioners need to show that the purchase of their legal practice will put the buyer in a stronger position than setting up from scratch. In chapter eight, Shelley Dunstone of Legal Circles, who has guided many sole practitioners through the sale process, demonstrates how sole practitioners can secure and enhance the value of their practice to prospective buyers. She discusses the options available to sellers, the saleable assets, and how to evaluate the worth of a practice including an in-depth look at the value of goodwill. The chapter concludes with a checklist of ways practitioners can maximize the prospects of selling their practice and getting the best price. However a sole practitioner chooses to sell, this chapter shows how planning ahead will ensure long-term success for the retiring solicitor and their practice.

Succession and retirement have long been considered taboo topics in law firms. Our final chapter, penned by Ronnie Fox, who has over 50 years of experience working as a solicitor, and is now developing a career as a retirement counsellor, takes a broad view of succession in the legal profession. Having seen many lawyers and law firms struggle with retirement and succession issues, Ronnie outlines five underlying reasons why lawyers and law firms find it so difficult to deal with retirement and succession, offers five ideas to help lawyers address these challenges, and five solutions to these critical problems.

About the authors

August J Aquila, CEO of AQUILA Global Advisors, LLC, specializes in compensation plan design, mergers and acquisitions, partner accountability issues, and succession planning for professional service firms. He has advised PSFs for more than 30 years. He is the author of more than ten books on professional service firm management, marketing, pricing and partnership issues. He has worked with clients in India, the United Kingdom, Canada and the US and has written hundreds of articles. He was a former partner in a top 50 accounting firm in Chicago, Illinois and an executive with American Express Tax and Business Services, Inc.

Jaap Bosman is an award-winning strategy consultant and an investor. After having spent 15 years in legal practice, he founded TGO Consulting, a highly successful consulting boutique that works globally with elite law firms and premier legal departments. Jaap is a seasoned consultant and widely considered one of the world's thought leaders on the business of law.

His achievements have been recognized in 2013 by the *Financial Times* with the first ever Innovative Lawyers Award for International Strategy. He is also a winner of the Thomson Reuters Excellence in Legal Marketing Award.

Jaap has published three books and many articles:

Death of a Law Firm (2015). This book is about the business of law and the human dynamics that drive it. *Death of a Law Firm* has become an influential global bestseller.

Data & Dialogue – a relationship redefined (2019); co-authored by Vincent Cordo. This book is about the relationship between law firms and clients. It introduces revolutionary new concepts such as the Value Matrix© and the Creation-Production Divide-Concept©.

A New Dawn (2020). This book outlines in hands-on practical terms how the legal industry could emerge better and stronger after the COVID-19 induced economic crisis.

He regularly contributes articles to leading publications around the world.

Sandra J Boyer is the founder and president of Legus International. Described as "a key visionary in the legal industry", she works closely with the Advisory Board to provide forward-thinking education, management, administration, and marketing programs that help the organization go above and beyond the traditional network model.

She is the co-author of Associate Retention: *Keeping Our Best and Brightest* (June 2002), and *The Effective Associate Training Program, Revised Edition* (2006). Both books are published by the American Bar Association's *Center for Continuing Legal Education*. She is the co-author of *The Survival Guide to Implementing Effective Law Firm Management Strategies*, published by the Law Practice Division of the American Bar Association (2015). She is also published internationally regarding timely law firm management topics.

For almost 30 years, Sandra has consulted with small to mid-size law firms in all areas of law firm management. In 2003, Sandra was inducted as a Fellow of the College of Law Practice Management in recognition of her outstanding contributions and sustained commitment to the highest standards of professionalism in law practice management. She received the Olivet College 1844 Award for outstanding commitment and success in her professional life as well as her commitment to Olivet College and its goals and strategies.

Shelley Dunstone is an Australian lawyer and the founder and principal of Legal Circles, a consultancy practice that helps lawyers achieve their business and career aspirations. Shelley is a past chair of the Senior Lawyers Committee of the International Bar Association. She was admitted to legal practice in 1981 and is a former law firm partner. She also holds qualifications in marketing. She provides coaching and professional development services for lawyers throughout Australia and internationally.

Ronnie Fox of London law firm, Fox & Partners, specializes in the law and practice relating to employment and partnership. In 1998 he founded and became the first chairman of the Association of Partnership Practitioners, which helped win recognition for partnership law as a distinct area of expertise. Major independent guides to lawyers and law firms have said, "Unparalleled in his experience", Ronnie Fox "has seen it all and done it all many times before, and knows the path of least resistance out of every situation". In relation to employment law, "Ronnie Fox commands a strong reputation for his work on senior executive departures and restrictive covenant matters". Ronnie's name continues to command instant recognition in the partnership sphere as an "admirable, vastly experienced practitioner who never loses his energy", and a "perfect choice for major issues and big, bet-the-partnership disputes".

Ronnie has written a book on termination payments, edited another on *Partner Retirement in Law Firms*, and contributed chapters to six other law books. Dozens of his articles have been published. He is a past chairman of the IBA Senior Lawyers' Committee.

Law firms and individual solicitors turn to Ronnie for advice, particularly lawyers whose love of practicing law makes difficult any meaningful discussion of retirement and succession.

Hermann Knott is an experienced transactional and dispute resolution lawyer based in Cologne, Germany. He is a member of both the German and the New York Bar and a partner with KUNZ Lawyers, where he leads the international practice. After attending law schools in Germany, Switzerland, and the US, Hermann started his professional career with a New York law firm where he was involved in US investments in the post iron-curtain world. After some time with a German internationally-oriented firm practicing corporate litigation he was a founding member of Andersen Legal, the law firm associated with the global Arthur Andersen organization. Aside from his transactional practice, Hermann has developed a focus on alternative dispute resolution, i.e. mediation and arbitration. He also has considerable experience in law firm management issues, having been the co-chair of that Committee of the IBA and the ABA International Section.

Pam Loch is the managing director of Loch Associates Group and has been a specialist, award-winning employment law solicitor for over 20 years. Unusually, she is a dual qualified solicitor, with degrees in accountancy and economics as well as law. She has combined her business experience and her legal expertise to set up a group of businesses that includes Loch Employment Law and HR Advise Me. Alongside her team of lawyers, HR consultants and wellbeing experts, she provides strategic and creative solutions for clients, managing the tougher side of their business operations for them so that they can sleep at night, knowing they are in good hands.

Pam is a seasoned commentator on the TV and radio, regularly called upon to discuss employment law and HR issues as they emerge. As well as contributing to books, she writes articles for many publications and media outlets including International Workplace, People Management and *HR Director*. She is also ranked as a Leading Individual in employment law and her firm is a Leading Firm too.

Over the last 30 years, **Veronica Mann** has built up vast expertise in all aspects of wealth creation, including retirement and protection. This, coupled with her in-depth knowledge of lifestyle planning, has helped her clients to secure their own financial independence.

This is particularly important for people going through life-changing events – such as retirement, bereavement, or divorce. Veronica focuses on helping her clients understand what they want from life. She also helps them to answer the crucial question, "Will I run out of money?". Knowing this enables her to develop plans so her clients know what needs to be done in order to achieve and maintain a comfortable and financially secure position, particularly in their later years. Veronica is both a chartered and certified financial planner and an accredited member of the Society of Later Life Advisers. Prior to this she has been the owner of a family company which developed a unique road safety product, a chartered surveyor, and director in her own independent financial practice.

Susan Saltonstall Duncan is the founder and president of RainMaking Oasis. For over 35 years she has provided management consulting and coaching services to more than 160 law firms, professional service organizations, and hundreds of individual professionals.

Her consulting firm works with firms, practice groups, and individual lawyers on firm and practice/sector strategy, succession planning, client relationship management and development, client feedback and needs assessment programs, leadership coaching, business development training, coaching and strategy, lateral integration strategies, firm values, visions and culture and innovation.

Susan has served in in-house roles including director of professional development, director of business development and as chief strategy officer for a Global 25 law firm. She was inducted as a fellow into the College of Law Practice Management (COLPM) and into the Legal Marketing Association's Hall of Fame. She has widely published in legal publications, is regularly quoted in the press, and speaks for national and international associations. She is the author of *Building Enduring Client Loyalty: A Guide for Lawyers and Their Firms* (Globe Law and Business, 2021).

Chapter 1:
Creating and implementing a law firm succession plan

By Sandra J Boyer, president, Legus International

What is a succession plan?

A succession plan is a set of guidelines for transitioning attorneys into retirement while simultaneously transferring the service of existing clients and guiding firm leadership development. Succession planning is vital to the continuation of the firm. Plan formality varies depending on the culture of the law firm. Firms that create and implement a succession plan have a competitive edge. Well organized succession plans benefit the retiring attorney, the firm, and the firm's clients. A comprehensive succession plan must be carefully created, but the implementation can actually be even more impactful than simply the creation of a documented plan.

An effective and comprehensive succession process considers both the transition of firm management and firm clients from the current generation to the next. Neither element is necessarily more important than the other; however, it is crucial to remember that both elements contribute to the successful continuation of the firm.

A comprehensive succession plan focuses on:

- Creating an effective management and leadership transition program to ensure current leaders help train and develop future leaders; and
- Creating a win-win-win (firm, lawyer, client) transition program that assists current firm clients to remain with the firm after the retirement or unexpected departure of primary client attorneys.

The importance of a succession plan

Firms that create and implement a succession plan are far more effective in transitioning both the management of the firm and firm clients. When developing a succession plan, firms evaluate their current professional staff, encourage senior attorneys to share their retirement plans, determine the effect of those retirement plans on the firm, develop a timeline for retirement of those attorneys, and outline a plan of action to ensure that management transition is effective.

Once the plan has been developed and implementation begins, it is important to consistently monitor the process and the plan to ensure it is accomplishing its goals. Also, at least annually, the responsible person or group should review the plan, anticipate upcoming retirement considerations, and ensure the plan can still be effective based on firm circumstances. The development, implementation, and monitoring of the plan is not a one-time effort, but must be consistent and organized.

Investing in the creation and implementation of a comprehensive succession plan is a sound venture with a strong business case. Benefits include:

- Enhancing the firm's ability to attract quality clients;
- Retaining quality clients on a long-term basis;
- Improving the firm's ability to attract high quality lawyers/partners;
- Retaining the high-quality lawyers/partners the firm benefits from;
- Promoting the maintenance of strong, long-term firm financial health;
- Providing consistent high quality, highly skilled client service;
- Developing new firm leadership/management while maintaining continuity; and
- Ensuring the long-term success of the firm.

Elements of firm management transition

Management transition programs vary depending on the structure and culture of the firm. Acknowledgment and analysis of the firm culture provides the basis for creating a program that has buy-in and can be successfully implemented.

Culture can have a direct impact on the development and implementation of the firm's transition plan.

If a firm is a first generation law firm, many times the founding leaders of the firm have maintained control of vision, planning, and financial strategies and have not included the next generation in any management processes. This top down management can make it very difficult for the founders to train and include the next generation of leaders. If the firm culture has been inclusive, it is much easier to understand, accept, and implement a leadership transition in the best interest of the firm.

When developing a management transition it is important to understand what strategies can work best within the firm and based on its culture.

Involving the next generation of leaders in management early in their careers is one consistent element of successful transitioning. Training young lawyers in management after two to three years of experience with the firm allows for the development of career paths for the next generation. There are several ways to integrate young attorneys into the management activities of the firm. For instance:

- When they join the firm, help them develop as a leader by assisting them in creating a practice and development plan. The goal is to become a good lawyer. Evaluate that plan with them annually. This helps them focus and grow consistently.
- At appropriate times, and with appropriate guidelines, the firm should share the business of the practice of law, including firm financials, with them. This helps them understand business operations. Partner compensation or other personal information would not ordinarily be included in the information provided to associates.
- After two to three years, begin to involve them in firm committees and assign tasks. If the committee has a budget, include them in the budgeting process. This allows the firm to observe their abilities to get things done outside the substantive practice of law.
- Involve them in the recruitment of associates. They could also be involved in the process to identify new attorney needs. In this way, they can understand how firms decide when and who to hire.
- Designate them as the “manager” of the paralegals within the firm. They can be responsible for organizing and coordinating the work, developing systems, and assisting in the evaluation of paralegals. They can serve as the “go to” person for questions from paralegals. This helps them gain people management insights and skills.
- Involve them in the development and implementation of the firm’s orientation and training/mentoring program. Having been through the new lawyer process, they can provide feedback and input to enhance the current program or develop a program where one is not present.
- Involve them in lunches with clients. This enables them to watch, develop, and implement various marketing strategies, and involves them in the client development and marketing aspects of the profession. They can learn from senior attorneys and begin to develop a sense for which rainmaking methods they would feel comfortable implementing.

Perhaps the most critical element of a succession plan is how to identify those younger attorneys who demonstrate the skills and abilities needed to become effective firm managers. The detection of these skills can start with the lawyer recruitment process and should continue through their employment. In order to prepare younger attorneys for management roles, they must first be identified as having the personality or ability to manage people. They must also have the ability and skills needed to become effective managers.

To recognize young lawyers with management qualities, firms must first decide what skills they seek. To do this, they should create a description for each of the management positions in the firm filled by lawyers. The description would establish the duties of the position, the qualifications, and the skills necessary to meet the demands of the role. Often, firms review the skills and abilities of current successful leaders within the firm and try to emulate those characteristics in their associate hires.

At the outset, consider all young attorneys as possible candidates for management positions, then eliminate those lawyers who do not meet the leadership and management criteria as outlined in the position descriptions. During the evaluation process, the associate's committee work, marketing ability, skills demonstrated, and any other important specifics should be considered.

Firm managers are leaders of the firm. They must possess the ability to gain support for ideas, build relationships with others, and gain the trust and respect of those they lead. When identifying future leaders, management can also consider the personality of candidates. Consider questions like: *Does this person have the respect needed? Does this person treat others with respect? Does this person treat staff with dignity?* Answers to these questions are essential in determining if the candidate will someday be a leader of the firm.

If the firm has an active training and mentoring program, the mentors should have a good sense of the skills of their mentees. The mentors should be aware of the firm leadership and management criteria and compare those requirements with the qualifications of the young attorney they are mentoring, then provide input regarding whether these mentees are developing the skills necessary for future leadership positions.

Management transition is not a one-time event, but a continual methodical process with focus, planning, and implementation. Remember, when developing future leaders who can effectively assist in the firm succession plan:

- The succession of the firm starts when you hire an attorney.
- Start early in an attorney's career.

- Be consistent and organized.
- Put somebody in charge of young attorney leadership development.
- Hire quality attorneys who meet the firm criteria of leadership.
- Assist in building their leadership and management skills.
- Evaluate them annually to ensure progression.
- Give authority where appropriate for success.
- Understand firm culture and ensure young lawyers fit into it.

While transitioning firm management must focus on the future and who and how it will be addressed, it is also important to work with and respect the attorneys who are transitioning out of management positions. They most likely have contributed greatly in the years they have been involved in management. A good management transition plan should assist current firm management to transition, whether it is to a more full-time practice or to retirement. Managing a law firm is time-consuming and stressful. It is not what attorneys are trained for in law school and it is often over and above practicing law.

The transition plan should include steps for those leaving management, which could include:

- Creating a billable hour step up program if they plan to remain in practice. This would allow for transitioning attorneys to begin to build up their book of business and billable hours over a specific amount of time.
- Work with the transitioning attorney to develop a "personal practice plan" that will act as a roadmap for their future, either with the firm or in retirement.
- Determine if the attorney can act as a "mentor" to management, especially if the firm faces challenges where experience and knowledge is required from those who have spent years in management.
- Determine if the transitioning attorney has a special or unique ability that can still be used by the firm in a less time-consuming manner.
- Work with the transitioning attorney to ensure they can provide input to firm management, just as any other partner can, without it being the conclusive voice and threaten the success of the new management team.

Elements of transitioning firm clients

Shifting clients is not an individual responsibility but a firm responsibility. To effectively transfer clients from one generation to the next, the retiring attorney must work together with the firm to ensure the clients receive quality and consistent legal services throughout the transition process. Both the individual lawyer and the firm must be committed to client retention before, during, and after the retirement of the primary attorney.

Long-term elements may include:

- Effective training and mentoring programs for young attorneys. This prepares the next generation of primary attorneys for clients.
- Creating teams and assigning them to each client. The team would include the primary attorney and a secondary attorney or associate. This helps maintain client communication if the primary attorney should become unavailable.
- Client education. Work with the client to let them know the firm is mentoring and training attorneys beyond the primary attorney. This helps the client/firm relationship continue. The firm can create a promotional packet to be shared with clients regarding qualifications of attorneys, the teams available to serve them, etc.
- Involve younger attorneys with clients in various situations – social, business, in court, etc. The firm can create a bank of training hours focused on assisting young attorneys in developing without the worry of not meeting their billable hour expectations.

Focused elements may include:

- Review the firm's roster of top clients on a regular basis – preferably every two years – as well as the primary attorney for that client. This will enable the firm to be familiar with the client base as well as who is responsible for each client. The firm can then identify clients who will need to be transitioned at any time.
- Create a timetable for the transition of clients once the firm is aware of a retiring attorney. This process should begin at least five years in advance of the end date for the retiring attorney.
- Identify the attorney who will become the primary attorney for the clients.

- Create a transition compensation program that helps to reward the retiring attorney and the attorney who will become the primary attorney. This provides incentive to participate in the transitioning process without penalty.
- Identify what the retiring attorney might receive beyond compensation as they transition out of the firm.
- Work with the retiring attorney to identify the role they will play, if any, in the firm after their retirement.

Remember, when implementing an effective client transition plan:

- Plan – don't wait until the last minute.
- Identify the younger attorneys with whom the client is comfortable.
- Begin the transition before the client understands it is happening – use the team approach to client service.
- Keep the current primary attorneys comfortable and anxiety-free.
- Avoid negative consequences for the retiring attorney – they are a very important part of the process.
- Select the appropriate replacement lawyer and train early and consistently.
- Ensure open communications between the retiring attorney and the firm.[1]

Impediments

Creating and implementing a firm succession plan is not easy. To be better prepared, identify the obstacles the firm might face. Some of those obstacles may include the following.

Firm management

- A lack of interest in the firm's future.
- No clear understanding of current roles in management.
- Attorneys lacking the time to devote to mentoring and training regarding business operations.
- Current firm management being reluctant to involve the next generation in discussion and decision making.

- The current management structure limiting the roles to a few attorneys.
- Attorneys unwilling to serve in management roles as it takes away from their client work.
- Attorneys not being rewarded for management roles.

Client transition

- The firm's complacency regarding the relationship between the responsible attorney and the client.
- Attorneys who are uncomfortable with other attorneys in the firm performing legal work for "their" clients. It is also true that clients sometimes do not want attorneys other than their "point" attorney to work on their files.
- Firm attorneys not being familiar with the business of the retiring attorney's clients.
- The primary lawyer providing poor legal services to the client and the firm not being aware of the problem.
- Primary attorneys who horde clients.
- An ineffective transition compensation program.
- Not identifying the attorney who will become the primary attorney for the clients.
- The primary attorney unaware of their own client's needs, short-term and long-term.
- The primary attorney being unaware of a leadership transition within the client business.

Additional considerations

Financial

It is important for a firm to include financial planning as part of the firm's succession plan for the retirement of primary attorneys and the shifting of their clients. This part of the plan can be flexible as each situation of retirement could be different; however, having general guidelines is important.

As retiring attorneys begin to transition, their established level of compensation may decrease, which can cause them stress, as well as the firm. It is important for the firm to recognize this and work with the retiring attorney to create a fair and equitable process. Ceding client control is difficult for many retiring attorneys, so based on the change in compensation and the transition of client control, many attorneys can be hesitant to begin the retirement discussion.

Creating and implementing the firm's succession plan enables the firm to be organized and prepared. It sets an expectation of what the process includes and how it will affect the retiring attorney and the firm. A well-managed firm is far more able to handle these circumstances when they arise.

Some financial considerations include creating and implementing a compensation/benefit program for the retiring attorney as well as the new primary attorney. Both compensation packages must include incentives for the retiring attorney to transition their client as well as the new responsible attorney to take on the work. The firm must understand how many retiring partners are actively moving through the transition at any given time and ensure the firm balances payouts to revenue generation, capping it per year as needed.

An example for retaining clients of a retiring partner:

Year one: Fees from the retiring partner's clients: retiring partner receives 40 percent, firm receives 40 percent, and working partner receives production credit up to 20 percent of fees.

Year two: Retiring partner receives 30 percent, firm receives 50 percent, and working partner receives production credit up to 20 percent of fees received.

Year three: Retiring partner receives 20 percent, firm receives 60 percent, and working partner receives production credit up to 20 percent of fees received.

Year four: Retiring partner receives 10 percent, firm receives 70 percent, and working partner receives production up to 20 percent of fees.

Year five: Firm receives 80 percent and working partner receives up to 20 percent of fees received.

This is only one example of hundreds of options concerning the financial portion of the firm succession plan.[2]

Communications

Creating buy-in among attorneys is also vital to the success of the firm succession plan. To create buy-in, ask attorneys to participate in the development of the plan. Many firms survey their attorneys for input during the development phase, then ask for feedback once the draft program is developed. The final succession plan is then communicated to all attorneys and implemented accordingly.

The transition of clients will not happen if the retiring attorneys don't buy-in to the succession plan or feel they are not supported by the firm. Open communication regarding the process is essential.

The transition of a law firm from one generation to another must take into consideration the differences between generations. What may have proactively made the firm a success with the past generations may not carry through to the new generation. It is imperative that firms understand the differences regarding work/life balance, flexible work schedules, virtual communications, work strategy, office "face" time, desired compensation, etc. Trying to force the transition of leadership and clients to do "what has been done before" can have adverse effects on the overall transition of the firm.

Conclusion

Developing and implementing law firm succession plans is time-consuming and difficult but it is much easier than dealing with the disorganized, reactionary process that might be the alternative.

Transitioning firm management, developing future leaders, and transitioning firm clients requires active participation and investment from not only the retiring attorneys but everybody in the firm. Open communication regarding succession goals is imperative to success. A focused approach is essential. Early and organized planning leads to a more orderly transition.

References

1. See Chapter three: Holding on to clients when senior partners retire for more information on client succession.
2. See Chapter six: How to compensate retiring and retired equity partners for more information on compensation considerations in succession planning.

Chapter 2: Succession planning considerations for the senior lawyer

By Hermann Knott, partner, KUNZ Lawyers

Introduction

It is never too early to think about succession. That is true in any enterprise or non-profit entity that has one or more leaders, unless it has only been established for a limited purpose. Another obvious truth is that law firms – although organized in a corporate structure and benefiting enormously from technology – offer personalized services. Law firms are often chosen because of the substantive and personal qualities of the acting lawyer(s). That element of course plays less of a role when choosing large or even global firms. In that context, it is often more the reputation of the firm that causes clients to select it, rather than the qualities of the individual lawyers.

Where individuals are strong their departure leaves a hole, unless efforts are made to prevent this early on. Succession is an issue for firms of all sizes. The smaller the firm, the more acute the issue is, as it may affect the very survival of the firm. The issue is exacerbated by the fact that successful lawyers typically are also emotionally engaged in their work. This passion – which is such an important factor in our profession – makes one easily neglect the fact that all our work and capabilities will come to an end at some point and that one is better off making an early effort to start managing that situation. Thinking about how the next generation will appreciate one's life's work should also not be neglected. We live on in how we are remembered.

With this context in mind, it is the purpose of this chapter to take a closer look at the perspective of the senior lawyer in firms of all sizes on how to best approach succession. I would not be a lawyer without raising a note of caution at this stage: the individual circumstances are so manifold that no standard solutions can be offered. And we should be grateful that this is the case. With each succession we face unique and individual circumstances. Taking them into account contradicts the application of standardized solutions.

Another aspect to consider is that a chapter like this is of course influenced by personal experience. In this context I have witnessed the discontinuation of a firm in my own personal environment as well as seen many other situations in which succession was an issue. This was particularly the case when I was involved as an officer in the Law Firm Management Committee of the International Bar Association and the Practice Management Committee of the American Bar Association in the 2010s. I have been co-chair of both Committees, giving me the privilege of a broad-based experience in issues affecting the operations and strategic orientation of law firms. My main practice, though, has always been client work, achieving solutions that help them continue in a better way than before. I spent a long period of my career working in a large law firm, and have recently joined a medium-sized firm.

Types of succession

There are various ways in which succession can occur:

- There are successors in the firm who continue to run the firm as a result of internal growth;
- The firm can merge as an equal partner with another firm;
- The firm could be "sold" to, or absorbed by, another firm;
- The firm could recruit a team to be the successors, who would then continue the firm's identity; and/or
- The firm could "buy" or otherwise integrate another firm.

There is obviously a wide range of ways to establish succession. Which solution to choose and how to manage the process, in particular whom and how many to involve, depends on the circumstances. The most important ones are the size of the firm and the stage of the career of the person who needs to be succeeded.

The importance of timing

As with many important stages in life, having to do something under time constraints is neither desirable nor necessarily guarantees the best outcome. Therefore, especially in a smaller firm environment, early planning or having one or more successors is important. Succession is a natural part of life. We all think about who our heir should be.

A sole practitioner, for instance, although having a number of staff, may take the deliberate decision not to have their firm continue when they cannot work anymore. That is a legitimate decision outside the scope of this chapter. If this is not the case, in his or her mid-50s he/she will ask himself or herself: *I need to bring in a successor who may benefit from today's still strong and active clientele, and I may get some support for my retirement. At the moment he/she will enjoy the benefit of entering a firm with the good reputation I have built over the years. So if the required competences and the personalities match, then this is a perfect solution, and I can gradually reduce my heavy workload of the last three decades and concentrate on more strategic issues aimed at securing the future and broader position of the firm.*

It is to be recommended that the senior lawyer seeking succession avoids being faced with a situation in which it becomes imperative to take a decision. Such an objective is the result of the long-term nature of succession planning. This holds true in law firms as much as it does in any business enterprise. Lawyers' work on the one hand very much depends on the quality and the personal engagement of the individual. On the other hand, specialization, the impact of technology, and the volume of documentation in matters of some significance require a team of people with different competencies and levels of experience to be involved. Therefore, even for a sole practitioner with an interest in handling more than just small cases, there is an inherent need to have several people working for the firm leader.

The structure typically is a bit like in the Chambers of Barristers: like the barrister the sole practitioner needs an "infrastructure". In the Chambers this infrastructure is provided on a shared basis by the Chambers to all members. In a sole practitioner firm the team only works for one firm, although models of sharing overhead services is certainly something that smaller firms should envisage introducing. A significant difference lies, however, in the fact that in the Barrister's Chambers the only lawyer is the barrister, whereas given the tendencies described above sole practitioner firms easily develop into firms with more than one lawyer. This raises the possibility of a successor developing out of that junior role. That may be the case even though the senior lawyer did initially not intend such development to happen. That is a situation I would call the "Unintended Successor Model". Unfortunately, this is not the situation occurring in the majority of cases. If the opportunity of an unintended successor arises, the senior lawyer may miss the chance, as he/she may be fixated on an external solution without realizing the available talent.

Sole or lead practitioners in small firms in any case pose a great risk for the firm and all its people. Should they become unavailable permanently or for an extended period of time, then the firm is bound to discontinue its work unless it can be "sold". For someone thinking ahead (including

– or especially – the employees who may have less social protection than the owner) this poses a permanent latent risk. This is one reason to start looking for successors early.

Success can be the greatest inhibitor to change. If the sole or small practitioner is successful, why bother with change? Add to that the fact that often these firms are built on the success of one or more individuals with strong characters who are not used (nor willing) to share. Sharing, giving something away, or facing the prospect of giving something away, is inherent to succession. That idea is often not favored and put aside until the last moment.

Impact of the size of the firm

As we have seen when discussing timing, the size of a firm is a crucial factor in the succession process. Large firms have an institutionalized process of transferring responsibility. That process applies to multiple areas of leadership, starting with the managing partners, other firm leaders, and continuing with practice group and sector leaders, as well as office heads. The starting point of the process of selecting the person taking over a leadership position in a large firm is the mandatory retirement age. Especially in Anglo-Saxon firms, this age is relatively low, for two reasons: one being the young age of entering professional life, and the other is based on making career development more attractive by clearing the way for new partners to join other than as a result of growth alone.

The latter is an important aspect for the career decisions of both junior and senior lawyers. In the legal profession, experience and highly developed personal skills are valued greatly in rendering client advice. Therefore, in many cases, partners should not leave the firm too early, as their experience is what makes them such a good lawyer. On the other hand, such a system gives junior lawyers a guarantee that their career development is not delayed by senior partners hanging on to their positions (and partner units). The issue of retaining the experience of those senior lawyers is, however, not the subject of this chapter and is discussed in chapter four.

It is clear that in larger firms the process of handing over responsibilities to other lawyers occurs at an earlier age, applies to more individual lawyers, and is usually more structured. In smaller firms it often occurs at a later age and is less structured, not least because smaller firms have either no retirement system, or one that is more flexible or allows for retirement at a more advanced age.

Smaller firms should, however, not ignore the recruiting aspect of the succession model that they apply – if they want to recruit at all, of course.

In many jurisdictions we are experiencing limited expansion of the legal market in total with growth prospects for law firms largely resulting from offering terms that are superior (in whatever respect) to those offered by competitors. Therefore, succession may also be an element of larger efforts of often smaller or medium-sized firms to improve the competitive position of the firm as a whole. Of course, such unplanned changes of leaders for urgent reasons also occurs at large firms. It may also be the result of sudden death or other incapacitating events occurring to the leader.

Preparing the next leaders

Up to now we have addressed the process of managing the transfer of responsibilities to new leaders. I would now like to embark on how the individuals can be best selected. Once the need for succession has been recognized and (more importantly) personally accepted, the senior lawyer and his or her partners should prepare a list of criteria they consider relevant.

Outside advice by an experienced independent adviser can be very helpful once the selection committee has made its first assessment. Leadership selection criteria are of course strongly influenced by the strategic view that the selection committee has adopted regarding the future direction and position of the firm compared to its competitors. Also in this regard, an external adviser is of great help. An independent adviser can inquire of the firm's clients and other stakeholders about their expectations and recommendations regarding the firm's future development.

An important consideration is the type of training future law firm leaders should have to prepare them for new roles. An able leader often displays a natural talent for leadership, which should be developed by entrusting gradually expanding tasks to him or her. In parallel, training in soft skills, accounting, and technology-related aspects are of additional value. Many leading institutions around the world offer specialist training courses on law firm leadership, which are essential in terms of exchanging experience with peers from other countries and cultures. Such training courses are especially useful for leaders in international firms or firms with an international reach.

Conclusion and outlook

Succession happens in all business enterprises. Particular attention needs to be given to the specificities of the legal profession and the character of law firms as service providers. In large and international firms, succession is a continuous process as it occurs on a regular basis, affecting the many positions for which new leaders are required.

In medium-sized and smaller firms the process is a rather extraordinary measure, typically involving all partners and affecting several positions in the firm. It is true, though, that these positions may be less clearly defined than in firms with corporate-type structures.

Especially for medium-sized and smaller firms the succession process offers an opportunity to combine the process with a strategic review of the firm's position in the way described above.

Chapter 3:
Holding on to clients when senior partners retire

By Susan Saltonstall Duncan, president, RainMaking Oasis

Introduction

Baby Boomer partners have been and will continue to retire in large and disproportionate numbers. Given how tentative many relationships are today between law firms and their clients, the threat of losing clients (and revenue) when partners retire is significant.

The best approach to long-term stability in a client base is to inculcate succession planning into talent and client lifecycles, not to treat it as a one-time transaction at the end of a partner's career. Firms that institutionalize clients consider succession less of an issue because numerous capable lawyers have been introduced to clients throughout the lifetime of the relationship. In these firms, no client relies on a single partner. Having good client transition plans and policies in place will be critical for firms as the disproportionate number of Baby Boomers retire. Firms can easily be de-stabilized if they lose client revenue so the goal is to ensure that both clients and the firm are well served during and at the conclusion of a transition period.

As with all other aspects of client and relationship management, the successful transition of clients must include active communication and engagement with the client. Too often, firms wait too long, select a successor and announce the decision to the client. This is a major mistake as clients must have a say in who their relationship successor will be. Clients know and worry that senior partners may be nearing retirement, and in the absence of any proactive outreach and conversation, may begin to make assumptions and start transitioning work to other firms.

This chapter provides a framework for helping firms improve the likelihood that they will be able to retain important client relationships and the attendant revenue as senior partners approach retirement. Components of the framework include:

- Following a consistent approach to client transitions for all partners;
- Getting a clear idea of which clients are at risk;
- Developing deeper and broader knowledge of each client;
- Engaging in important discussions with clients about satisfaction and succession;
- Considering and choosing the right successor; and
- Developing, executing, and monitoring a transition plan for each partner and each client.

Establish a uniform policy for retirement and succession

Set a required retirement age in the partnership agreement, or at least some milestones when partners must begin to map out client transition plans. You can still build flexibility into this by including metrics and other factors by which the management committee will review each partner on an annual basis and extend full equity partner privileges. For example, the firm could extend a partner's mandatory retirement for up to three years if several specific criteria are met each year. If the firm doesn't already require an annual business plan from each partner, ask every partner to establish goals for his/her practice that include a transition strategy.

Identify clients potentially at risk and assess relationship breadth and depth

There are two areas of data the firm can use to assess which clients the firm may be at risk of losing when a senior partner retires. The first is the firm's data on top clients by revenue. The second is a demographic look at partners and key client contacts aged 55 or older and the nature of relationship depth the firm has.

As to client data, do a three-to-five-year analysis of those clients that represent 80 percent of the firm's top 80 percent client revenue and break each client revenue into revenue by service or practice area. Analyze to see which partners, practices, and offices have been engaged in matters with clients and the nature and degree of contact. This will give you a sense of how well the firm has grown the client beyond the single relationship partner.

Since client relationships and relationship management often are even more critical than expertise in maintaining long-term loyalty with clients, it will be important to understand the depth and breadth the firm has with top clients. This can be done by developing a relationship map or matrix for each client that includes key members of the client's team matched to the firm's partners and associates. This will help the firm get an idea of where the relationship gaps or risks may be. In addition to looking at lawyers who currently are working on active matters, also look at the firm's customer relationship management (CRM) system to identify other firm lawyers and personnel who have relationships with client contacts.

It will also be helpful to do an assessment of the client's succession picture – soon to retire leaders, next generation stars that are being groomed, etc. It is common for general counsel to move to new companies and positions every three to five years, so the firm must take into account the continual shift in current and upcoming leaders. The relationship matrix of all known individuals in the client organization should include:

- Their titles/roles/responsibilities;
- Who else in the firm knows these individuals;
- Nature/depth of each relationship; and
- Current/future role each plays in the decision-making process.

Gain better knowledge of clients

It is important to develop a central repository of information for each client served by partners who may transition in three to five years. (Actually, this is good practice for all key clients that represent the top 80 percent of the firm's revenue.) This will include gathering important information about the client and the firm's relationship with the client, such as:

- Financial data for the history of the client to assess trends and services utilized.
- A relationship matrix that identifies and matches firm lawyers' relationships with different members of client organization (see prior section).
- An organizational chart that depicts the company's internal structure, including business units, operating units, and, most importantly, roles, responsibilities, and reporting structures.
- The client's annual plan and reports, 10Ks, 10Qs.
- The client's panel of law firms and procurement policies.
- Client outside counsel and billing guidelines; client preferences for work product, milestones, communications.
- Competitive intelligence report to see what other firms are on record as representing the client for litigation, business transactions and advice, regulatory compliance and intellectual property.

- Market research on client industry and competitors.
- An assessment of the client's future legal needs, growth strategy, and industry trends.

The current relationship partner, together with others in the firm that serve the client, should meet to review the information, discuss any concerns or obstacles, and identify specific issues to raise with the client as well as needs and opportunities to explore.

Talk to each client to gauge client satisfaction, loyalty, and any concerns

Proactively engaging with clients to understand their satisfaction with the firm, what their future needs may be, and gauging where your relationship stands now, is critical to do at this juncture. If the firm has not already implemented a regular client feedback program, send someone other than the relationship partner to meet with the client to solicit feedback on how well the firm is serving and meeting the needs of the client. This is also an opportunity to discover which additional lawyers in the firm the client most trusts (if they do) as well as other firms and lawyers the client relies on to gauge the depth of loyalty the client may have to other firms or partners. There is little point in developing a detailed plan to transition the client relationship until the firm is certain that it is fully meeting client needs now and exceeding expectations.

Clients often fear the retirement of a senior partner but are reluctant to voice their concerns to the individual or the firm. This is especially true if a senior partner has had a long-standing relationship with a company over multiple in-house leadership changes and has developed deep institutional knowledge and loyalty. Make clients aware of your efforts to continue to meet their needs and the firm's desire to keep serving them in the coming years. By implementing a plan several years in advance, the managing partner will have the opportunity to check in with clients a few times a year to evaluate how well the transition plan is working and to make adjustments as needed.

Carefully select client relationship successors

Decades ago, a partner who brought in a new client most often also did the client's work. Today, it is likely that the "billing partner" or relationship partner may be substantively engaged in some of the client's work but may also be overseeing and supervising multiple other partners and associates in the same or different practice specialties. The role of relationship partner has gotten much more complex and demanding in recent years and this often compounds considerations of who will be the right choice to ensure continuity, satisfaction, and loyalty in the next generation.

Firms that focus on developing institutional clients and that treat succession as developing a pipeline of talent to succeed the senior generation over many years enjoy smoother client transitions. In these firms, there likely already are multiple and meaningful relationships between the client and numerous lawyers in the firm.

Partners and firms have made many faulty assumptions and mistakes when considering succession of client relationships, including:

- Rainmakers have put into place one or two "deputy" partners to help manage the client's substantive work and assume that as subject matter experts, they also will be able to take on the role of relationship partner;
- Designated "deputies" or successors have been chosen in the "likeness" of the senior partner without regard to considerations of age, race, and gender and who might be a better relationship match for a client; and
- A partner has retained such close control over a client relationship that, once retirement nears, there is no one in the next generation that is a good fit to become the successor.

When considering to whom and how to best transition a client to the next generation, the client must be what drives the selection of a successor. Clients usually have a number of concerns when it comes to the transition of work and the relationship to a designated successor. Firms therefore must consider the following when considering successors:

- Will the partner be as responsive, accessible, and committed to the client as the originating partner is?
- Does the successor meet the client's desire for more diverse lawyers leading their matters and the relationship?
- Is there good chemistry between the active client contacts and the primary firm lawyers?
- Is the partner credible and credentialed in the eyes of the client?
- Does the partner have good judgment and understanding of the client's broader business needs and goals? Can she or he serve as a trusted advisor?

Ideally, client successors should be introduced into client matters five to ten years before a partner retires, but certainly no later than three years. Potential successors should be discussed with the firm managing partner to align firm goals and priorities with the right talent. In some instances, two partners will have to serve as successors – one who is more of the trusted advisor, has good chemistry with the client, and is designated as the relationship partner, and the other (or several) who might be a top subject matter expert in the client's industry. Whereas traditional rainmakers used to play the dual role of the general trusted adviser and the practice specialist, it is rarer to find this today in a single partner. This is why in many instances two partners may be chosen to serve as successors. In other instances, firms have not been able to find the right blend of expertise and relationship chemistry within their existing group of partners and may have to hire laterally to find a successor who is a good fit.

Once the designated successor(s) has been identified and the internal team has met to discuss the client (even if the team is just the current relationship partner and the successor), the relationship partner should meet in-person with the client to discuss his/her plans and to discuss the proposed successor. Ideally, the client has already met and worked with the chosen successor and has a familiarity and comfort level with the partner, but this is not always the case. Asking the client for input on the successor selection is critical.

Put a client development and transition plan and process in place

Centralized client management is something that clients themselves want from their outside law firms. Client teams not only ensure better and coordinated service to and more consistent and ongoing communication with clients, they formalize an approach to institutionalizing clients to ensure that there are multiple relationship touchpoints and opportunities for binding loyalty between numerous lawyers in the firm and numerous contacts at the client. Once a successor relationship partner has been identified (see above), that partner will assume responsibility for leading the client team, perhaps with the help of another partner or counsel with deep ties and history with the client.

Using knowledge collected about the client, the relationship matrix, and feedback from client interviews including the client's needs, the new successor – together with the retiring partner – should build an annual client action plan with the team to include steps to strengthen key relationships, entertain the client, provide continuing legal education (CLEs) via seminars, webinars, workshops and trainings, introduce other lawyers and practice areas, and engage in *pro bono* projects and charitable activities with the client. This is primarily a plan for internal purposes, but the client-facing plan might include discussions on pricing, when and how the firm and client will engage in ongoing debriefs, end of matter feedback and continuous improvement. The team should put together a mini-directory of the lawyers and other professionals dedicated to the client, which includes photos, contact information, and areas of expertise. Additional staff engaged with the client might include those in client development, pricing and accounting, knowledge management, paralegals, and practice assistants. This directory should be housed on the firm's intranet and also shared with the client on a client portal. The client team should meet on a quarterly basis to review progress in each of the areas in the plan.

The senior partner and the successor should be implementing a gradual transition of the relationship. This will include having the designated successor begin scheduling and leading meetings, sending the bills, and soliciting feedback on the firm's servicing of the client. The managing partner should also meet with the client several times during the two- to three-year transition period to gauge how well the transition is going so that any issues or concerns can be addressed. This is a critical phase of the transition as the client may be assessing whether or not this is the time to make a change in outside law firms. It is best to encourage open and honest dialogue in order to make any course corrections necessary, which in some cases might even include changing the successor. If the client is generally happy with the choice and how things are going, the successor should be accelerating efforts to deepen the relationship, loyalty, and value enhancement. Successors often benefit from some coaching from the relationship partner and some training on client relationship management, financial, leadership/team management, and interpersonal skills.

To effectively transition relationships, retiring partners will have to take an active role in introducing and promoting successors into the relationship. In the first year, the successor should attend all meetings, be asked to join calls, and be regularly cc'd on all correspondence, most likely at no extra charge to the client. By the second year, the successor should be playing a more central role in initiating calls and meetings with clients and even take on the billing responsibility. By the third year, the retiring partner may be included as an adviser and sounding board but not as substantively essential to matters. Members of the client team should also be making better and deeper personal and professional connections with members of the client's team.

If senior rainmakers are still contributing substantially to firm revenues, they likely are being well-compensated for their originations, for supervising hours and for working hours. In order to incentivize them to begin handing off and sharing credit for clients and matters, the firm should not penalize partners by decreasing their compensation or perks during a well-planned transition phase. As long as goals and specific milestones in the transition plan are being met, the transitioning partner should continue to be as well compensated during that time.[1]

Monitor progress to make sure the transition plan is working effectively

Once a formal succession process has been put in place, firm management (either the managing partner or department/practice group leader, along with the firm's CFO) should begin to assess actual transition metrics. This can be accomplished by:

- Meeting with the successor to review the partner's business plan, which addresses individual client transitions and gauge actual progress; and
- Reviewing metrics – working hours on client files by successor, transfer of origination, or billing/matter credit.

Since succession planning can be challenging for senior partners and firms alike, any successes in specific succession transitions should be communicated, recognized, and rewarded. One firm has added a column to its online individual partner dashboards dedicated to transition metrics, which indicates the hours/billings a senior partner has transitioned to a successor. In this scenario, the compensation system rewards both partners – the partner doing the transitioning/transfer and the successor.

The managing partner should have quarterly reviews with partners during a transition phase, especially since many partners naturally and understandably are reluctant to wind down and to give up control of relationships. During the active transition phase, the managing partner should also be having regular conversations with each client to gauge both the transition and overall client satisfaction.

Client transition checklist

- Establish firm policies and protocols for important client transitions.
- Run a report on partners aged 60+ who are associated with key client relationships.

- Analyze highest revenue clients to identify all partners that have relationships with and have worked on their matters.
- Collect additional information and background about the client and hold in a central repository for all client team members to access.
- Identify other partners who can continue to service these clients as well as those who might be a good fit for the client in other areas or in relationship attributes.
- Meet with clients to gauge their needs, any concerns they have, and identify the skills/traits that clients want and need in the successor; explore their preferences for diversity in those who lead the relationship as well as those on the team.
- Ask senior rainmakers what characteristics they are looking for in the right successors, helping them broaden their scope beyond those they might assume would take up the mantle.
- Identify additional potential candidates to be successors if needed; mentor and provide skills development in client relationship, client management. and finance/billing skills (all the skills required to effectively manage a "client account").
- Develop and execute a client transition and development plan.
- Bring potential successors to client meetings; foster familiarity for client so the transition is seamless.
- Conduct client interviews throughout the client lifecycle.
- Continually introduce clients to other partners and practice areas throughout the engagement to expand relationships and loyalty.
- Implement a more intentional recruitment effort to improve gender and ethnicity representation to break the cycle of unconscious bias in selecting successors.
- Have management check in with key clients, two to four times per year during critical rainmaker transition years, to ensure the client is confident in and happy with the successor and client team.
- Provide a financial incentive to begin the transfer of client relationships and track and recognize those who do so.

References

1. See Chapter six: How to compensate retiring and retired equity partners for further information.

Chapter 4:
Succession of rainmakers

By Jaap Bosman, founder, TGO Consulting

Law firm royalty

Achieving the status of rainmaker is as high as one can get within a law firm. Rainmakers have a special status. Nobody wants to upset them and their opinion weighs heavily when it comes to strategy and decisions. No rainmaker will want to lose this status.

Having an optimal and smooth succession in place when it comes to rainmakers is top priority for any law firm. Rainmakers attract a lot of work, have a great reputation in the market, and are highly trusted by their clients. Firms certainly don't want all this to get lost once the rainmaker leaves the firm. The firm will want to continue relationships with their clients after the partner has left. From the client's perspective there should preferably be little or no interruption in relationship and services after a partner leaves.

Partners whose revenue is in the upper ten percent of their firm are commonly considered rainmakers. If you have 30 partners in a law firm then 20 of those will generate an average turnover and about five partners will bring in a turnover noticeably below the average. The remaining five lawyers will be responsible for three times more turnover than the bottom five: the rainmakers. Being one of the highest contributors to the turnover, and presumably to the profit, gives someone clout in any company. In law firms, because they consist of a partnership, they become "royalty".

At some point every partner has to leave the partnership. Whether through advanced age, reaching the contractual retirement age, or by leaving mid-term, every partner leaves. Ideally, law firm partners beyond a certain age should gracefully "fade away", leaving their practice and address book to the generation below. Every once in a while, there invariably is a partner that refuses to facilitate that transition. These partners go out with a bang, causing lots of collateral damage.

When it comes to the succession of those partners that contribute more towards reputation and turnover, a bit more attention is required.

Managing a successful succession of a rainmaker requires planning, clever psychology, and time. Lots of time. It takes time for the successors to prove they are worthy of the client's trust. It takes time and planning to help a successor build a solid reputation in the market. It takes clever psychology to make a rainmaker open-up his/her relationships and accept and introduce successors.

Real rainmakers and fake rainmakers

The general assumption is that rainmakers generate high revenue, thanks to their amazing reputation and/or acquisition skills. However, in reality this is not always the case.

Some partners that have the rainmaker status within a firm have simply "inherited" a large part of their practice from a partner before them. Unless they cannot live up to the standard, these clients will typically remain loyal. In such cases, there is little or no acquisition skill involved. Building one's practice on a high quality "inheritance" is much easier than building from scratch. Succeeding a renowned partner will also be a definitive advantage in building a reputation.

There are also partners who just got lucky once on landing a very large mandate, maybe even because another lawyer was conflicted. This is especially known to happen in litigation. After a few years of high turnover, nobody remembers the origin of the riches and the partner has been crowned as rainmaker.

Some rainmakers go to great lengths to get files put in their name. Sometimes partners claim that they are the client partner, even if other partners do the actual work. Or, in cases where the matter came in under another partner, they make sure to open a second file in the same matter that is under their name. These "rainmakers" are rainmakers because they are very protective when it comes to their book of business, not necessarily because of their great acquisition skills.

Reaching the status of rainmaker by gaming the system in this way is detrimental and cannibalistic to the firm. It doesn't actually bring more and better mandates by attracting them from the market in competition with peer firms. It merely reshuffles internal revenue flows and detracts attention from the fact that it is not benefitting the firm, especially since these types of rainmakers tend to hinder further expansion of talent. They tend to only allow new partners to be appointed in their practice area on the condition that they will not compete and focus on a different segment of the market. What's more, such "rainmakers" purposely create weak offspring by appointing their "helpers" to partner while expecting them to keep serving in their practice. We know of many instances where so-called rainmakers never made partners that were better or equally good as themselves.

Above are just a few examples to illustrate that not every lawyer who is perceived as being a "rainmaker" actually possesses the magical skills required.

Hostages and Stockholm Syndrome

Being a rainmaker almost invariably includes having an important voice when it comes to the management of the firm. Rainmakers rarely act as managing partner, but behind the scenes they want to pull the strings. This as such might seem logical, but it actually does not make sense. The qualities that make a rainmaker are different from those needed to define the strategy or to manage the firm. So why is it that rainmakers wield so much influence?

Many law firm partners will have experienced a situation where concessions are made to a top earning partner based on some form of implicit threat in making a rainmaker unhappy. Presumably this unhappiness could lead to the rainmaker leaving the firm and taking his/her book of business with them. These concessions result in allowing disproportional influence on the strategy, special or extra compensation, or exception to retirement rules, just to mention a few examples. As discussed, the highest-ranking firms in terms of profit per partner in today's market have a spread between the highest earning partner and the lowest earning partner of about three to one. In the past decade the average compensation spread among law firm partners has widened. Firms say they are constantly evaluating their compensation model to align them with strategy. In reality, systems are often tweaked to satisfy the current rainmakers. Putting rainmakers on a pedestal is a form of Stockholm Syndrome.

To understand why rainmakers have such influence that a law firm can be held hostage by an implicit threat to leave, one must understand how law firms work financially. As a guiding benchmark and as indicated in the introduction to this chapter, the highest grossing ten percent of a law firm's partners generate three times as much turnover as the ten percent with the lowest turnover. It is important to understand what this means in terms of potential damage to a law firm's profitability. Say that we have a hypothetical law firm with 100 partners generating a turnover of \$20,000 (this is just for the example, not a real-world figure). The top ten partners each generate \$300 which will be \$3,000 in total turnover while the bottom ten together generate \$1,000. The other 80 partners each generate the average of $200 and a combined total of $16,000. The market average of costs for a law firm is around 65 percent of the turnover. This cost is predominantly fixed in nature. It is for the most part salaries of associates and staff, and the rest are costs surrounding the office. Very little of a law firm's costs are flexible. Using the same example, the costs would be $13,000 out of the $20,000, leaving $7,000 in profit. If the top ten partners leave, this would decimate the turnover by $3,000, or by 15 percent. But the cost remains $13,000, which means that the $3,000 comes straight off from the profit, resulting in a profit loss of 42 percent. What was a profit of $7,000 is, with the swipe of only ten partners, reduced to $4,000. Few law firms will survive a 42 percent drop in profit.

In general, above average talented lawyers are more attracted to nicer work than nicer profits. The talented lawyers want to work with the other best lawyers in the market and will always seek the top end of clients and matters. This is the most stimulating environment as well as the highest form of recognition. Any moderate fall in profit will not lure them away. But if their peers are equally praised elsewhere and their fellow partners are not the very best in their legal field or do not have the business acumen to run the firm as befits a top-notch office, then a dip in compensation might well be enough to send a rainmaker looking. This delicate equilibrium of reputation and compensation is the most sensitive at the very highest end of the market.

Central to this hostage situation is the question of who owns the client relationship. A departing rainmaker will try to transfer his/her book of business to the next firm and might take all or most of his/her team if leaving. This will leave the old firm vulnerable and thus susceptible to any threat of a rainmaker looking for greener grass elsewhere. A partner can do this because law firms allow partners to monopolize a client relationship.

The relationship between a client and a lawyer is one based on people. It is the individual who over many years is able to build trust. It is the individual who makes the relationship. As law firms reward turnover or provide origination credits, partners are incentivised to keep tight control on client relationships. Having said that, some law firms have built a quality reputation that complements or exceeds the reputation of the individual partner. Such law firms have operational and cultural elements in place that strongly support the individual lawyer in meeting or even exceeding client expectations. Such law firms spend, for instance, considerable efforts on talent recruitment and training, ensuring each partner a great team. Any law firm that wants to increase the value of its brand should work on building a firm relationship with the client. A relationship that will continue to blossom even after the partner has left. Conscious and methodical succession planning has to be an important part of this.

If the disparity between a law firm's best partners and the rest of the partners is too great, then it becomes a rift that cannot be bridged. Law firms end up being held hostage by their top ten percent of partners or by one or two rainmakers with strong personalities. The hard remedy here is that keeping your best partners might not be the best thing to do. A split-up and a clear strategy going for another profitable segment may be the best path to take. It's a tough decision, but oftentimes a better option than being ruled by one or more individuals that may not have the best interest of the firm as a whole at heart. Such a firm will never be able to move forward and be a winner in tomorrow's market.

Santa's little helpers

Law firms are what we call talent breeding machines. In fact, it is one of their most strategic tasks. A law firm's entire engine is the skills and experience of its people. Making sure that there is always a solid supply of people that possess the skills of the required level or above is central to success. This is why, in the most successful firms, the investment in time and training of its associates is consciously made and continuously monitored. The leverage in these firms, i.e. the number of associates to the number of partners, is typically very low.

As mentioned, rainmakers are most of the time in firms where the spread between partner revenues is typically very high. After all, if everyone generates the same turnover then there would be no top earner. Of course, there can always be a difference between partners in terms of abilities to bring in new clients and attract new mandates but, if this is not coupled with the, by comparison, higher turnover, then prima donna behaviour usually does not follow. As mentioned previously, the problem with rainmakers is that they typically do not train associates to become the next rainmaker. They mould them to become a supporting role in their own operations. We usually say they tend to produce Santa's little helpers – diligent and careful lawyers that excel in producing the documents and make up for any shortfall that the partner might have. While this might result in a fantastic turnover, it hardly helps the firm with stacking the pipeline of future rainmakers. It might not produce any future partners at all. Santa needs the helpers and cannot do without, but they will never be the next Santa. Strong partners create weak offspring because it serves them well. This is a serious strategic flaw in the continuity or competitiveness of the firm in the medium- and long-term. For the firm that has not made partner succession part of its strategic agenda, the retirement of rainmakers is a major risk.

Retirement reluctance

Partners who are today hovering around the age of 60 started their career as a lawyer more than 30 years ago. The legal world in the 1990s is in many aspects incomparable with the legal industry today. During that timeframe the legal industry has seen exponential growth. The business of law has been professionalized beyond recognition, in part thanks to pioneers such as Harvard professor David H. Meister who published his book *Managing the Professional Services Firm* in 1993.[1]

Partner incomes have quadrupled and many partners are earning more today than they ever imagined when they became partner some decades ago. Baby Boomers have built their career with an incredibly strong tail-wind. Not only their professional career, but also in their private lives. For example, the value of their property has risen tremendously.

Not only thanks to their extraordinary talent, but also in no small part due to favorable circumstances, the Baby Boomers have built impressive practices with big revenues, high profitability, and a strong reputation in the market. Now that they are around the age of 60, they are starting to think about their future. Most law firms have set an age limitation to equity partnership. This age limitation has now come in sight. This is often causing sleepless nights for the partners concerned.

Today, no one around the age of 60 would consider himself/herself ready for retirement. Thanks to a better lifestyle and medical advance-ment, people are getting older and staying in great shape much longer. Any lawyer approaching their early sixties will still consider himself/herself fit for practice for many years to come, and rightly so.

But partners in law firms have to retire, not because they are old and tired, but because they have to make way for the next generation. Being a partner is different from being an employee. Partners have entered into a contractual relationship and in this contract is stipulated when it ends. It is a business arrangement, not a personal or emotional one. Whether or not the partner is still fit to maintain a high level practice at the age of retirement is not part of the equation. The contract ends, and that's all there is to it. Nothing personal.

Reality is, however, that most "senior" partners do not see it that way. They have developed a kind of amnesia as to why the partnership agree-ment is formulated as it is. When they were still young partners, it seemed like a great idea to set a fixed age limit to equity partnership and make room for younger partners to grow their business and their profit share. When reaching the age limit themselves, their perspective has completely shifted. Now it feels as if they are being cut off at the height of their career.

From a purely business perspective it is in the interest of the firm that partners start transferring some of their practice and clients early on. Ideally this starts as soon as the partner makes a new partner. New partners should get part of the practice as a form of "starting capital" the day they become partner. Splitting a successful practice in two is the most efficient way to grow revenue and profitability for a law firm. Around the age of 60 a partner should actively start to transfer mandates, clients, and reputation to the younger generation. The problem is that this requires a great amount of trust. Obviously the partner should have complete trust in the quality of the next generation. But if rainmakers have been allowed to make Santa's little helpers partners, the trust in the abilities of the next generation partners will hardly be there.

Sometimes rainmakers want to continue practicing until they are 70 or beyond. Rather than transferring their practice to the younger partners, these take their practice and move to another firm towards the end of their career. For them, not transferring their practice is part of an "insurance policy" that they still have market value.

But it is not only a lack of trust in the next generation and the fear of losing one's special status as "law firm royalty" that keeps a rainmaker from wanting to retire. Depending on the profit distribution system, financial motives might be a serious hindrance for succession. People are often surprised about how little planning partners do for their retirement. They simply haven't prepared well enough for an abrupt stop of income.

Mitigations

Management guru Tom Peters is probably the most famous consultant McKinsey has ever produced. His influence on the firm was enormous and helped raise McKinsey's profile beyond its wildest dreams. Yet, in 1981, Tom Peters was asked to leave. His contentious departure has been well documented. McKinsey had, and still has, a rule that the firm is more important than the individual. When Tom Peters became a "prima donna", McKinsey did not hesitate to "kill" its most celebrated rainmaker. And as we all know, it turned out that "firing" Tom Peters did not harm the firm.[2]

For law firms, the first step is to recognize the Stockholm Syndrome and to overcome the urge to allow the rainmaker to behave as a spoiled celebrity. Law firms could learn from McKinsey in recognizing that the firm is more important than the individual. Don't be afraid to part with a rainmaker that is wielding undue influence over strategy and the execution of it.

Secondly, and perhaps even more important, a law firm should consciously mange the quality of its partner group. The idea that rewarding rainmakers with extra compensation to keep them bringing in the business is based on the fact that not all partners are equally good at this. In fact, many partners are not good at bringing in clients and mandates at all. Yet, the ability to attract mandates and clients should not be an exception. It is a core requirement for every partner. Law firms are still focusing on legal competencies when it comes to nominating new partners. It should be recognized that commercial and relationship skills are far more important. Lawyers should be trained from the day they start to develop those skills. When the average quality of the partner group increases, the rainmakers will gradually disappear, as every partner becomes a rainmaker. Being a rainmaker should become the rule, not the exception. Then the creature will lose its royal status.

An equal partnership also facilitates smooth successions because it takes trust for retiring partners to transfer a practice. The partner must get the comfort and the guarantee that transferring part of his/her practice before retirement will not lead to loss of respect, status, or income.

The only way to mitigate adverse effects of lateral partner movement is doing a permanent risk assessment. Law firm leadership needs to map the relationships their clients have and help them to actively broaden this relationship. This could be done through introducing other partners, encouraging associates to build parallel relationships with the client on their level, having the managing partner visit the client periodically, or even having a good contact between secretaries or finance departments. Intertwining of IT systems is also an effective method. It is advisable to try and build multiple relationships in order to become less dependent on one person.

Finally, if the leadership is weak and a firm has appointed a management that are hostages and loyal subjects of rainmaker royalty, there is no hope in achieving smooth rainmaker successions.

Rainmaker succession, hands-on

As the quote, attributed to Alexander Graham Bell, goes: “Before anything else, preparation is the key to success”. Making sure that the retirement and succession of rainmakers will be as smooth and effective as possible is a strategic priority for any law firm. It is all about awareness and preparation. Having mapped the potential issues in this chapter, they can be boiled down to a number of mitigating measures.

- Preferably start ten years down the line by preventing partners being put on a rainmaker pedestal. Foster a collaborative and sharing culture among partners. Make it standard practice that each recurring client has at least two relationship partners. Don't allow partners to monopolize relationships. If done from the outset, no client will object.
- Don't allow partners to build a team of "Santa's little helpers" that are converted into weak partners at some point. There should be no such thing as "helper partners". All partners need to possess practice development skills.
- Every newly appointed partner should receive part of the practice of his/her mentor as a starting capital. Promoting an associate to partner should always include transferring some clients. Don't financially penalize partners for transferring part of their practice.
- Make a strong effort to promote young partners in the legal directories rankings to avoid reputational loss after the rainmaker retires.
- Make it a standard practice to prepare partners for retirement, starting five years before reaching the set age. This includes counselling on personal finance, social relationships, and personal relationships. This will help mitigate feelings of retirement anxiety.
- Be very strict on maintaining the set retirement age. Make no exceptions as even the slightest chance of being allowed to stay longer will promote "bad behaviour" and stand in the way of transferring clients.
- Be aware that all the above gets more complicated in an "Eat what you kill" profit distribution system. It is advisable to have a partner compensation retirement support pool, to in-part help compensate for the loss of income as a consequence of transferring practice.

References

1. David H. Meister, *Managing the Professional Services Firm*, Free Press, 1993.
2. Duff McDonald, *The Firm: The Story of McKinsey and Its Secret Influence on American Business*, Simon & Schuster, 2014.

Chapter 5: How to compensate retiring and retired equity partners

By August J Aquila, CEO, AQUILA Global Advisors, LLC

It's no secret that the legal profession is aging. Senior partners in many law firms are Baby Boomers; the oldest are in their mid- to late-70s. Around 60 percent of law firm partners are Baby Boomers, and 25 percent of all lawyers are 65 and over. Lawyers in their 60s also control 25 to 35 percent or more of the revenue in many law firms.[1] It's very likely that many of these senior lawyers will retire in the next decade, and the COVID-19 pandemic has only accelerated retirement plans for many.

While the debate around the lack of future partners and how firms are going to survive from one generation may never go away, firms also need to develop compensation plans to keep productive retiring and retired equity partners productive and on board. Firms are so worried about generational differences in the workplace that they tend to forget about the value of their senior or older partners.

I am not suggesting or recommending that unproductive partners should be kept in the firm. These partners should be dealt with immediately, no matter what their age. However, I am suggesting that we look at senior partners as valuable assets and determine how we can best keep them employed and compensated.

Senior partners possess a wealth of knowledge about the firm, client relationships, long-term referral sources, and the firm's oral history. Retaining this intellectual capital makes any firm stronger. However you decide to use senior partners, make sure it is a win for the firm and the partner.

Getting started

Make sure that your partnership agreement clearly lays out the retirement process. While you will want to keep some retiring partners on board, you do not have to keep all of them. Also, there is no single compensation plan that works for all firms. Every firm has a way they compensate partners. What is important is that partners who are in the transition phase are not penalized. As their roles and commitment to the firm changes, their new compensation should fit their new roles.

Key partnership agreement issues

Before we get to compensating retiring and retired partners, it's necessary for the firm to have a clearly stated retirement process in place. This permits the firm to proactively plan for succession, secures the transfer of client relationships from one generation to the next, and allows younger professionals to move up through the ranks. Today, many partnership agreements have a mandatory retirement age, which is usually 66 to 70 years of age. At that point in time, the firm, not the retiring partner, decides what happens next. Here are the most common options:

- The partner retires and leaves the firm;
- The partner stays on for an additional year or so as an equity owner; or
- The partner stays on for an additional year or so as an employee.

At the end of each year, the firm determines whether it wants to keep the partner in the new role, change the role, or let the partner go.

Retiring partners

Let's deal first with retiring partners. These are partners who will be reducing their workload in the next two to three years and then moving on to one of the three options mentioned above. With demographic shifts reshaping law firms today, many firms are struggling with the challenge of how to best compensate these partners transitioning to retirement. In many firms, senior partners represent a large percentage of the equity in the firm. They may also generate a large percentage of revenue and manage most major client relationships. If the firm doesn't have a plan to transition these partners, their clients, and referral sources, it is putting its future existence at risk.

Client transition

Retirement should not be a time when the firm and the retiring partner are at odds with each other. They both have a mutual interest and can greatly benefit one another by working together. A smooth client transition is as critical for the firm as for the partner. To ensure that this occurs, make certain that your compensation and retirement plan do not conflict with what you are asking the retiring partner to do – transition his or her clients to another member of the firm. If there is an inherent conflict in this situation – for example, if the firm is continuing to compensate a retiring partner on his or her billable production, but wanting the partner to transition clients without any compensation reward – the partner will not transfer the clients and the firm will miss out on a valuable opportunity.

Client transition normally takes one to two years. During this time, you want to compensate the retiring partners, not penalize them, for transitioning clients.

There are six areas that the firm should evaluate when transitioning clients from one relationship owner to another. The retiring partner should be compensated based on the fulfillment of these areas.

1. Identify key clients

Obviously, you do not have to worry about every client, but it is important to take care of your most important clients. If you have already identified clients as "A", "B", and "C" clients, then you have done a lot of the preliminary work.

When you identify key clients, you will want to consider the following factors:

- Annual fees;
- Legal services provided;
- Realization and profitability of the matter;
- Client reputation in the marketplace;
- Importance of client to your niche area; and
- History of client services and service peculiarities about client.

2. Identify key client advisors

Care must be taken when transitioning a client to a new service provider. The ideal situation would be to transition the client to another partner or senior associate who already has familiarity with the client. Having more than one person in the firm serving as a relationship manager is a foundational strategy for effective client transition. The retiring partner and the managing partner/executive committee should approve all transfers.

When you identify key client advisors, take into consideration the following factors:

- The individual's knowledge of the client and/or the industry/niche;
- The chemistry and personality of the new attorney with the client;
- The existing workload of the new attorney; and
- The willingness and enthusiasm of the attorney to take on the new client.

Never force a key client account onto another client service provider.

3. Communicate with the client upfront
It is important to involve the client in the transition process. This is usually a multi-step approach. First, the retiring partner informs the client that he or she will be retiring in the next two to three years. Second, as an important client of the firm, the retiring partner wants to make sure that the client continues to receive the same level of service they have been receiving. Third, discuss with the client the individual who may take over the account. Fourth, introduce the client to the new service provider so they become comfortable with the individual while the retiring partner is still with the firm.

4. Hold one-on-one meetings with the client
Key client accounts deserve and require a face-to-face meeting. This is an important time to inform the client of the upcoming retirement of the partner and get the client's input into the transition plan. As the new partner proceeds through the grooming process, all communications should be handled by the new partner. A post-engagement review is handled by both the new partner and the transitioning partner. Finally, the "new partner" is ready to handle every aspect of the client relationship while the retiring partner assumes a supervisory position.

5. First year follow-up meeting
It is important to have a follow-up meeting with the client either after six months or one year after the new partner takes over. This can be done by the managing partner or the firm's marketing partner/director. This provides the client with a vehicle to voice any satisfaction or dissatisfaction with the service or service provider.

Senior partners who are transitioning clients may have the following performance criteria to accomplish in order to receive a bonus.

Area	Goal	Weight	Actual results	Bonus award
Identify key clients	Identify top 20 key clients	25 %		
Identify new service providers	Each of the top 20 key clients have a new service provider identified by 20XX	25 %		
Communicate with client re pending retirement	75 % of top 20 key clients are notified	25 %		
Introduce new service provider to key clients	Introduce new service provider to 50 % of top 20 key clients	25 %		
		100 %		

Figure 1: Performance criteria for a senior partner's bonus

Retiring partners have fewer billable hours so their compensation goals should be adjusted accordingly. Here are some areas you may want the retiring partner to accomplish goals in. These may include training associates, helping another lawyer take over a practice area, or introducing referrals sources to the firm. Figure 2 below is an example of a retiring partner's performance compensation plan.

Area	Goal	Weight	Actual Results
Production	Reduce billable hours by XXX hours	30 %	
Client Transfer	Transfer XX % of clients by 12/31/20XX	35 %	
Leadership	Identify new practice area leader	15 %	
Subjective	Be a good firm citizen, follow firm policies, etc	20 %	

Figure 2: Performance compensation plan for a retiring partner

Creating options for retired partners

There are many meaningful ways to compensate senior partners whom you want to remain with the firm after they retire and no longer retain an equity position in the firm. Let's explore the top three:

1. Revenue generating options.
2. Non-revenue generating options.
3. Options outside the firm.

Revenue generating options

While there are partners that do not relish the daily grind when they get into their mid-60s, there are others who have the stamina and desire to continue working well into their 70s.

For marketing purposes, the retired partner may retain the title of partner but now works under a new compensation plan since he or she is no longer an equity partner or shareholder. The new compensation plan can be structured in many ways. For example, some firms will base it on a percentage of cash collected from his or her personal production. The percentage is usually between 30 percent and 40 percent. Other firms will retain the partner on a project basis and pay a flat hourly rate.

Many firms develop a part-time or flextime arrangement in which the partner only works when needed. The key to making all these options work is to ensure that the retired partner is no longer controlling clients that should have been transitioned to someone else in the firm.

If the retired partner's compensation is based on production, it is advised that it be based either on gross profit of the engagement or actual cash received. You should never compensate any lawyer based on billings.

Figure 3 below is a sample compensation template for a retired partner who mainly continues to bill for his or her own production hours.

Billable time	Billing Rate	Gross Revenue	Realization	Net revenue	Cash collected
1,000	$425.00	$425,000	87%	$369,750	$325,600

Figure 3: Retired Partner A

If Partner A is the sole producer of this work, then the firm pays Partner A between 30 percent and 40 percent of the cash collected ($325,600), or $97,680 to $130,240, not a percentage of the net revenue figure. Payment is made throughout the year monthly. Cash that is collected in the following period is counted and paid out then.

If Partner A is merely the relationship partner for the services, his or her compensation is based on gross profitability of the matter because other production people are doing the work.

Billable time	Billing rate	Gross revenue	Realization	Net revenue	Gross profit
1,000	$425.00	$425,000	87 %	$369,750	$221,850

Figure 4: Partner A – Relationship Partner

If we assume that the cost of services sold is 40 percent or $140,900, then our partner in this example would be paid a percentage of the $221,850, for example 35 percent of $221,850 or $77,647.50.

Non-revenue generating options

There are several ways that a former partner can add value to the firm other than billing clients. If you are lucky, your senior partner has developed a true expertise in a specific area and will be willing to develop younger professionals by acting as a coach or mentor. Other retiring partners might have a database of referral sources that can be used to continue to send new clients to the firm. Still others might enjoy campus recruiting, searching for merger candidates, or just helping with the firm's projects. All you need to do is identify specific projects that senior partners could add value to when they are no longer working for the firm in a full-time capacity.

If you pursue this option, partners are usually paid on an hourly or flat rate to lead certain areas in the firm. For example, one firm is using its retired managing partner to become the chief rainmaker in the community, while another firm has retained one of its retiring partners, who teaches at a local university, to head up recruiting. Once older partners are relieved of the pressures of being full-time producers, they often embrace these new roles with renewed passion. Instead of feeling disconnected because they are leaving a firm where they may have spent the last 30 years, they feel useful because they are still making a real contribution to the firm and to their community.

Some firms have a pay-for-performance compensation plan. The partner may receive a base salary plus the opportunity to earn a bonus that is set at the beginning of the year. There are many different types of pay-for-performance templates. The following is based on a Balanced Scorecard approach.

Area	Objective	Target	Weight	Actual Performance
Financial	Assist in the development of new client matters	$1m in new business	35 %	$800,000
Client	Create client satisfaction survey	Be approved by Executive Committee by end of 20XX	10 %	Not approved
Employee	Develop new associate on-boarding program	Operational by end of 20XX	20 %	Operational
Business Process	Explore ways to improve billing process	10 % decrease in billing time	35 %	8 % decrease in billing time
			100 %	

Figure 5: Balanced scorecard template – for representative purposes only

Let's assume the bonus potential is $40,000 and the partner achieved the above results in Figure 5.

1. $800,000 in new business: 35% × 80% × $40,000 = $11,200
2. Client satisfaction survey – not approved by the executive committee: 10% × 0% × $40,000 = $0
3. On-boarding program – operational: 20% × 100% × $40,000 = $8,000
4. Improve billing process – 8% increase: 35% × 80% × $40,000 = $11,200

Total bonus = $30,400.

Options outside of the firm

Many older partners serve as goodwill ambassadors for their firms. If your retiring partner does not want to continue with the daily grind of client service, that does not mean that he or she must stop being an asset to the firm. Many firms have outstanding alumni programs where former partners and employees continue to promote the firm.

The secret is that both parties develop a winning outcome. Law firms have been able to place senior partners in a variety of positions, including:

- On boards of local non-profit organizations;
- On boards of privately held companies or hospitals;
- As full- or part-time positions with one of the firm's clients or prospects; and
- Teaching at a local law or business school.

It is important to ensure that the retiring partner continues to be a loyal supporter of the firm. There is no better marketing tool than to have as many people as possible in the marketplace saying good things about your firm. Why not make your former partners some of those people?

The successor partner

Let's not forget about the successor partner. There are many variables that will impact this individual's future career and compensation – new role, new responsibilities, amount of business assuming, potential leadership position, and size of firm. There is not a single answer when it comes to how to compensate this individual.

Make it happen

Good things happen because we take the time to plan them out. Often, a retiring partner will want to ignore the fact that a life-changing event is on the horizon. Take the initiative and start talking with your senior partners today. Let them know that the firm wants to support them during this time of transition. As mentioned earlier, all partners need to feel good about the pending changes. Being honest and upfront regarding what the senior partner can expect in his or her new role will make it easier for a smooth transition to take place. Remember, retiring partners are valuable assets. You just need to find a way to make use of their full potential.

References

1. www.attorneyatwork.com/your-boomer-retirement-problem-wont-just-fade-away/

Chapter 6: Diversity considerations in succession planning: future-proofing law firms through diversity

By Pam Loch, managing director, Loch Associates Group

Note: To be clear, for the context of this chapter, a diverse workforce is made up of people from a wide variety of backgrounds and experiences, and may include age, ethnicity, religious and political beliefs, gender, physical abilities, and sexual orientation.

Introduction

While diversity and inclusion has remained on the agenda of governments worldwide, there is no doubt the COVID-19 pandemic has pushed it down the priorities. However, that could be about to change.

In the UK, the well overdue Employment Bill is expected to be published in 2022 and includes several measures deriving from the UK Government's 2018 Good Work Plan, which could impact diversity and inclusion at work. It includes extending the redundancy protected period for pregnant employees to six months after the pregnancy ends and expanding rights to paid time off for new parents and carers.

The Flexible Working Bill is also expected to take effect in 2022, reflecting the increasing demand for flexible working across all sectors following the COVID-19 pandemic. It is well evidenced that certain groups of staff are likely to benefit from a flexible workplace culture – predominantly women (who are more likely to have primary caring responsibility for children and other dependents) and disabled workers.

With burnout and mental health issues on the rise, the culture of presenteeism that has been the mainstay of traditional law firms is also suddenly very much under scrutiny. At the same time, the demand for high quality staff has risen dramatically since the start of the COVID-19 pandemic, mainly due to large numbers of experienced professionals re-evaluating their work/life priorities – and law firms are far from immune.

Law firms, along with businesses from many other sectors, are now facing the real risk of not being able to attract and retain the specialist expertise required to fill their business-critical roles. Law firms need to start thinking now about how they can sustainably transform their business to create a more diverse and inclusive workplace, or risk losing valuable talent to more inclusive competitors, as well as increasing their exposure to reputationally damaging discrimination claims.

This chapter discusses the issues law firms should consider when scoping out their diversity agenda, highlights the pitfalls of getting it wrong, and offers some tips and tricks to successfully future-proof their firm through succession planning in an increasingly diversity-led culture.

Issues facing businesses around lack of diversity

When it comes to sustainably transforming a law firm into a more diverse and inclusive workspace, it's imperative to first evaluate and understand the current situation. When it comes to generally evaluating diversity within the business sphere, there are undoubtedly a number of issues that need to be addressed.

Firstly, evidence suggests that there is a real lack of diversity at senior levels. Consider the following facts: only 3.2 percent of executive and senior management positions are held by black employees,[1] while only one percent of these reach CEO at Fortune 500 level companies, and all of them are men.[2] In these same companies, there are fewer CEOs who are women than men in leadership positions who are named John.[3]

Although 57 percent of employees think their company should be more diverse,[4] a recent report noted that 41 percent of managers are "too busy" to implement diversity initiatives.[5] This is further confirmed by the 40 percent of people who believe there is a double standard against hiring women,[6] although research shows that teams where men and women are equal can earn up to 41 percent more revenue.[7]

In UK law firms, the Solicitors Regulation Authority has reported[8] that the prospects of becoming a partner are higher for white males than any other group across all types of firms. Entry into the profession is diverse but female, BAME, and disabled lawyers continue to be underrepresented at partner level. BAME and disabled solicitors are proportionately more likely to work in smaller firms, whilst high-street firms give BAME males, white females, and BAME females the greatest opportunities to become a partner. BAME women are particularly disadvantaged in progressing within the solicitors' profession.

These stark statistics highlight the urgent need for a considered diversity agenda in today's modern workforce. The pitfalls of getting this wrong can lead to a number of issues for law firms, including fewer allies for discrimination victims, limited perspectives in the workplace, and fewer role models.

Further driving these issues is a rapid shift in dynamics. "Baby Boomers" – the largest generation the world has ever known – are either now fast approaching retirement age, or are already enjoying early retirement.

In the United States, recent research[9] has shown that roughly 50 percent of the government workforce is eligible to retire now, whilst one in five of all senior executives in the Fortune 500 are also eligible to retire. Further to this, NASA has predicted that 25 percent of its staff will reach retirement age within a matter of years.[10] Current trends also demonstrate that the average college graduate is likely to change jobs five times in their career – a number that is set to increase to seven within the next ten years.

With startling statistics such as these, businesses across the globe – including law firms – are recognizing the challenges of recruiting and retaining leaders. This has only been exacerbated by COVID-19, with many people now re-evaluating their work–life balance, and questioning how much responsibility and stress they are willing to take on in order to progress in their careers.

How can businesses address these issues?

These are issues that clearly ought to be addressed – and fast. However, the challenges presented provide opportunities for businesses to diversify and embrace fresh talent. So, how best to address these issues in a timely manner that will ultimately benefit the business?

One of the best ways to attract and retain talented people across a diverse pool is to offer growth opportunities within the firms that they might otherwise seek in other places. Numerous studies have shown a clear correlation between organizations with diverse leadership teams and business success.

Succession planning could be the answer to this.

Succession planning

Succession planning is a strategic way to find talented individuals to fill roles within an organization. Specifically, it is the ongoing process of identifying future leaders within a business and developing them so that they're ready to move into leadership roles when the time comes.

Rather than following the usual approach of placing adverts and making phone calls to find candidates who are unhappy in their current roles – or rushing to find someone in the two-week notice period of a departing employee – succession planning focuses on sourcing the right person, rather than just the available person. This is the difference between replacement hiring (reactive) and succession planning (proactive).

Succession planning is described as having the right people in the right place at the right time and should take the place of replacement hiring in any law firm that hopes to compete for the best talent in the workforce.

This form of planning has evolved over the years. Once, it was reserved for the last wills and testaments of family-owned companies, and later expanded to include companies who planned to replace CEOs. Now, instead of such a narrow focus on replacing the top few positions, the strategy is being implemented for leadership at various levels across an organization.

One of the benefits of this broader approach is that it encourages succession plans that can embrace diversity, equality, and inclusion.

Diversity considerations in succession planning

In 2019, more than half of diversity and inclusion (D&I) leaders identified succession planning as a top priority, which is no surprise given that racially diverse teams have been shown to outperform non-diverse teams by 35 percent.[11] As this kind of research continues to show how diversity and inclusion can contribute to enhancing performance and company culture, businesses are realizing more than ever that a homogenous succession plan can actually pose a significant risk to long-term profits. The sense is that a lack of different perspectives fails to provide a fully comprehensive solution and might potentially create a hostile environment that contributes to a higher turnover of staff.

From May 2020, calls for racial justice following the Black Lives Matter movement accelerated companies to immediately evaluate their diversity and inclusion practices, particularly at the top level. For example, the former founder and CEO of Reddit resigned from his position on the company's board in the wake of the movement.[12] He has now been replaced by Michael Seibel – an entrepreneur who has been active in promoting diversity efforts among start-up founders.[13]

So, when it comes to succession planning, much data and research proves that the most successful plans are developed by a team of representatives from different levels and areas of the organizations. By using various representatives, it is possible to establish a broader understanding of the organization to ensure that the plan meets the true needs of the business – not just those perceived by one group.

How to: succession planning

It is key that succession planning is utilized as a business strategy and enforced by a specific team. A group of carefully selected people will determine the success of the project, and the future of the workforce. As such, it's imperative that people are chosen based on the contribution they can bring to the process, rather than just their seniority or job title.

In some companies, the succession planning team is composed only of the senior team. By expanding the team's composition to encapsulate diversity, businesses can help to ensure that there will not just be carbon copy managers across the board. For example, ensuring that an HR representative has a seat at the executive table should improve the balance between data-driven and people-centric decisions around talent management. In larger corporations, there may also be shareholders who should have a say too, whilst in smaller businesses and family-owned companies, the succession planning team may include different generations of those involved.

There are a few basic steps in the succession planning process, and the planning team should ensure that diversity is considered at each stage.

1. **Assess the organization** – organizations that want to encourage diversity need to assess where they are, not only from a pure numbers perspective, but culturally. Is the organization primed for diversity? Does it value and uphold a climate of inclusion where there is safety to show up as one's authentic self? Is leadership valued at all levels of the business, and is there a culture of "belonging"?
2. **Determine key positions** – organizations that want executive teams with more diversity should start by outlining the roles and responsibilities that need to be filled. Analyze the opportunities for diversity and inclusion at every level to benefit from a range of perspectives.
3. **Identify competencies for key positions** – it's vital to ensure there are dedicated talent management opportunities for diverse populations, including transparent succession planning, with widely communicated goals, benchmarks, and competencies.
4. **Identify and assess candidates** – when considering internal versus external candidates, look to find out if there are already people with potential within the organization. There almost always will be. Assess them individually via a gap or basket analysis tool to reveal areas to develop in each person. Keep an open mind when thinking about potential successors and focus on the skills required versus their current role.

5. **Create development plans** – once candidates have been selected, work with them to create comprehensive plans to ensure they grow the skills needed to succeed in their future roles. Include them in strategy talks and help them acquire the leadership, management, and planning skills they'll need for the role.
6. **Measure, monitor, report, and revise** – by continually auditing these practices and fostering an inclusive and diverse working environment, these cultural attributes will not only attract top talent, but also retain it.

Crucially, the time for succession planning is not when an employee leaves the law firm, but when a new starter joins. From their first day, they should be observed and coached to determine whether they are a potential leader, and to evaluate where they may need to develop to fulfil that potential. This is another example of why it's important to recognize diversity in the initial hiring process.

The global workforce is becoming increasingly diverse, and businesses that wish to be successful and ensure their continuity should reflect this global diversity. Companies need to be proactive and systematic about ensuring that their succession planning is truly inclusionary, diversified, and equal. But how best to do this? There are a number of pragmatic considerations to successfully future-proof a law firm in the increasingly diversity-led culture.

Benefits to business and future-proofing in an increasingly diversity-led culture

By creating an increasingly diverse workforce, law firms will experience a number of positive changes that will ultimately benefit the business in the long-term.

Firstly, by enforcing an inclusive and diverse company culture, the public perception of the company is likely to improve. As the public – and other businesses – latch on to this example of a forward-thinking and innovative company, recommendations and endorsements may increase, creating business revenue from new clients. If nothing else, the positive PR from diversity initiatives helps to grow brand awareness and build a positive reputation among the public and potential new clients.

In addition, and leading on from this, having a good reputation will create a much more attractive employer brand, showing the firm in a favorable light to prospective new employees. Having a solid reputation as an inclusive employer is likely to make attracting a range of talent easier – particularly in the current climate, which is a candidate driven market.

Using succession marketing to increase the quality of employees means that the firm is creating a brighter future for itself and seeding potential new leaders for the business.

A diversity-led firm will not only find itself with a better quality of potential future leaders, but also experience a whole host of other benefits. These might include enhanced creativity through greater individual expression, better employee retention through a happier and more inclusive team, improved innovation from a greater plurality of ideas, and a better understanding of clients from a more representative workforce.

There are other, more tangible, benefits to taking steps now to future-proof a law firm's diversity by developing all available talent. Perhaps the most attractive of these is the ability to access new income streams. By demonstrating a commitment to diversity through the workforce, firms can begin to develop deeper cultural links, and become a more visible presence within local community groups.

Proactively home-growing junior talent into business leaders is often the most cost-effective way of planning for a seamless succession into senior partnership roles. Crucially, it also brings with it individuals who live and breathe the firm's philosophy, and are personally invested in its progress. Increasing diversity in senior roles creates role models, and therefore inspiration for junior lawyers from minority groups. A greater pool of diverse talent should then develop through the ranks spontaneously, without the need to resort to high-risk positive discrimination tactics or quotas. Once begun, diverse succession therefore becomes the default.

Conclusion

There's never been a more important time to implement succession planning within a law firm – particularly one that encourages diversity and inclusion – as a new generation of employees emerges post COVID-19.

Today's workplaces are brilliantly diverse, and this diversity should be represented within law firms via succession planning. By enacting changes both within the planning team and in future leaders, firms can ensure that no group is excluded from participation in leadership development opportunities. This diversity also ensures fair and equal representation for all people in leadership roles for the firm.

Without diverse representation, there is an increased likelihood that the business will continue to perpetuate the status quo of the demographics of the leadership team – and without those different backgrounds and perspectives, the firm loses the opportunity to develop and grow with the wider evolving workforce.

References

1. https://coqual.org/wp-content/uploads/2020/09/CoqualBeingBlackinCorporateAmerica090720-1.pdf
2. https://fortune.com/2020/06/01/black-ceos-fortune-500-2020-african-american-business-leaders/#:~:text=The%20only%20black%20woman%20to,who%20stepped%20down%20in%202016.&text=That%20means%20that%20black%20CEOs,the%20most%20recent%20government%20estimates
3. www.nytimes.com/interactive/2018/04/24/upshot/women-and-men-named-john.html
4. www.glassdoor.com/employers/blog/diversity/
5. https://builtin.com/diversity-inclusion/diversity-in-the-workplace
6. www.pewresearch.org/fact-tank/2017/12/14/gender-discrimination-comes-in-many-forms-for-todays-working-women/
7. https://connectusfund.org/18-advantages-and-disadvantages-of-diversity-in-the-workplace-cultural-and-gender
8. www.sra.org.uk/globalassets/documents/sra/research/risk-business-case-diversity.pdf?version=4a1ac3
9. http://45.114.134.178:9000/digi/IG01/2007/IG01T00611.pdf
10. *Ibid.*
11. www.mckinsey.com/business-functions/organization/our-insights/why-diversity-matters
12. www.businessinsider.com/reddit-cofounder-alexis-ohanian-steps-down-2020-6?r=US&IR=T
13. www.redditinc.com/blog/reddit-welcomes-michael-seibel-to-board-of-directors/

Chapter 7:
Financial aspects of succession planning: protection and retirement considerations

By Veronica Mann, chartered financial planner, Talis Financial Advisers

Introduction

Traditionally, law firms have been structured as partnerships or sole practitioners. Today, some firms work as a limited liability partnership, which offers many of the benefits of a traditional partnership but with a greater degree of personal protection for the partners, and more recently some firms trade as limited companies. How you operate will affect the actions you take here.

You've worked hard all your life and now wish to exit. Ideally you started your working life with a view to exit and have built up some value, so that someone will pay for your share of a firm. However, many solicitors have a transactional business model with few significant repeating retainer fees.

The objective of a well thought through succession plan could be to retain the continuity of the business for the remaining partners or shareholders. It could also provide an exit route for the key players – which is of paramount importance if you are a sole practitioner.

Initially, the development of a successful succession plan must start with an understanding of who the key individuals in the firm are and their existing client relationships. Smaller firms or sole practitioners will be at greater risk because their legal expertise is concentrated within a fewer number of people.

Yet most firms have done very little to protect themselves from this loss. Unsurprisingly most individuals have also ignored this element of their own personal financial and succession planning to allow a safe and comfortable retirement.

I propose to look at some of the concerns for the firm and the individual, in order to allow the succession plan to be financially successful. Please note, this chapter has been written with a UK focus.

Figure 1 shows some of the things that can get in the way of a successful plan. You will note the similarities for the firm and the individual.

For the firm	For the individual
Unexpected exit of the key player	Changes in the structure of the firm
Poorly drafted contracts	Poorly drafted contracts
Death of a key player	Death
Illness of a key player	Inability to earn through sickness
Retirement of a key player	Retirement
Availability of affordable PI insurance	Claims in retirement

Figure 1: Impediments to a successful succession plan

Communication and contracts

One area where everyone has "control" is good communication and the substance of the contracts, which is vital to an efficient succession.

The first element of a good succession plan is to have a clear partnership agreement or director/shareholder agreement in place. This should cover the aspects of how a partner/director/shareholder retires and the relative remuneration strategy, as well as how the value of the practice should be agreed/calculated.

It is worth noting that a good partnership agreement should also ensure that the partners have a separate pension provision so that their income does not "suddenly" cease.

With limited companies, a properly drafted shareholders agreement will also cover the mechanics of the exit strategy/retirement of a shareholder and agree a valuation method to allow the purchase of the shares. In a company, the employer is obliged to provide some pension facilities. It is still down to the individual to maximize their pension contributions within permitted allowances to provide for their income on exit.

Financial planning for retirement

Looking at the individual, the retirement/exit strategy may be to create a clean break or phase out over a period. If you are exiting to take up employment in another firm, the next part of this chapter is of less immediate importance, but nonetheless essential. If you are exiting in order to retire, then your earned income will cease and you will be reliant on the financial planning you put in place during your working life.

Pensions

Whilst you are working, the most tax effective way to provide for your retirement is to use a pension.

Some people will have, or have had, the benefit of defined benefit pension plans. These were offered by some larger companies and government employments (such as teachers and the NHS in the UK). They offer a guaranteed pension within the scheme rules and are generally no longer available.

Today, companies will offer a money purchase plan where the benefit depends upon the amount of contributions, the funds selected, and the growth in the account, to provide the retirement capacity for your older age.

If you are an employee, your company must provide you with an auto enrolment pension contract. The current contribution is eight percent of qualifying earnings of which at least three percent must be paid by your employer. The upper limit on qualifying earnings is currently £50,270 (2021/22).

Pensions offer you tax relief at your highest marginal rate on each contribution you make; so that if you pay £800 into your pension, it will receive a further £200 as basic rate tax re-imbursement, making a total of £1,000. If you are a higher rate taxpayer, you can recover any additional tax when you complete your self-assessment. This means the £1,000 contribution might only actually cost you £550.

Pension funds grow in a tax favored environment and are exempt from inheritance tax (in most cases). From the age of 55, you can access your fund, 25 percent tax free and the remainder can be taken as taxable income. This does not need to be taken in one hit and can be planned in accordance with your future needs and tax positions. Modern pensions allow you to leave any fund remaining at your death to your chosen beneficiaries – family, friends, a charity etc. They do not die with you.

You can contribute up to 100 percent of your earned income with a maximum of £40,000 p/a and if you have not used up all of your allowances you may be able to catch up on the previous three years "space".

The UK government has imposed restrictions, if you are high earner, to limit these generous tax breaks. High income individuals are defined as those with an "adjusted income" of over £240,000 for the tax year and "threshold income" of over £200,000. Should you fall within this category, the maximum you can contribute to your pension is tapered back, until if your income is over £312,000, when your maximum permitted contribution is limited to £4,000 per annum.

If your income is around these levels, financial advice is essential so that you can maximize your permitted pension contributions and not fall foul of the rules, which would incur a tax charge.

There is a further restriction in pension planning – the lifetime allowance (LTA). This is the amount that you can save within a money purchase pension contract without incurring a tax charge. This is currently £1,073 million. The rules with defined benefit plans are different.

Many lawyers will want to find additional ways to provide for their retirement after a successful exit.

Other savings areas – with tax benefits

The next place to save would usually be your ISA. You have an annual allowance of £20,000 and can invest across collective accounts, direct equities, as well as holding money in cash (which will guarantee you a loss). There is no limit on the value of an ISA holding and, if invested in AIM shares, it can be exempt from inheritance tax as well. Unlike pensions, all the proceeds from an ISA are tax-free in your hand.

You may invest in a collective account – where the fund manager selects investments across a market – or prefer to invest directly into equities, which are traded on the stock market. There is a mantra that says you should only invest in equities money which you are prepared to lose. In both cases, profits from the sale of the holding are subject to capital gains tax – which comes into play if the gain is greater than £12,300. Prudent planning may allow you to realize this gain each year and increase your savings tax effectively.

There are two other investments where you can obtain tax relief. First of these would be Venture Capital Trusts. You can invest up to £200,000 per annum into VCTs. A VCT invests in AIM shares and not companies on the FTSE. You can spread your risk by investing in more than one. A qualifying VCT will allow you to claim 30 percent income tax relief. This is relief – not reduction – so you must have sufficient taxable income to allow you to reclaim the tax. Another benefit is that any dividends received from a VCT are free from income tax and capital gains tax, providing it is held for a minimum of five years. Building a portfolio of VCT investments may allow you to create substantial tax-free dividend income in the future.

If your personal succession plan means selling your partnership or business, you will exchange an asset that was exempt from inheritance tax to one that is subject to inheritance tax once it reaches your bank account. The questions then become, what do you need for your own life or for your family? And how to invest those funds?

You could consider an Enterprise Investment Scheme – again, these are government-sponsored tax advantaged investments designed to encourage investment in small unquoted companies. EIS allow income tax relief of 30 percent on the investment, which can be carried back one year. They must be held for a minimum of three years to retain the tax advantages. An EIS benefits from business property relief and is currently exempt from inheritance tax after being invested for two years. An EIS will allow you to roll in capital gains that have been created within the last three years, meaning you can defer the payment of the tax.

Property

Many people look at including property as a means of providing for retirement both during and after work. This may create additional taxable income from the rent generated, noting that rental income may be variable and is not guaranteed. Property will be within your estate for inheritance tax calculations and the sale of the property will create a CGT liability, unless it is your primary residence (home). As mentioned above, you can shelter CGT within an EIS but this will then be inaccessible for at least five years.

Death and incapacity of key players

The value of a law firm depends heavily upon the partners for leadership, ongoing client relationships, reputation, and sometimes the capital that funds the business. The loss of a partner or key fee earner/employee could have a dramatic effect and might even scupper any succession planning / merger negotiations that are ongoing.

The initial sale of *The Muppets* was cancelled when Jim Henson suddenly died in 1990. He was in negotiations with Walt Disney for a reported $150m. However, Jim Henson's children sold the company to the German media company EM.TV for $680m in 2000.

The retention of key members of your firm can be enhanced through additional employee benefits and protections offered within their employment terms. Pensions and life cover are the most common. The one that is most often overlooked is key person insurance. Both LLP and limited companies can establish key person insurance, which will provide a lump sum to the business (or the member) to mitigate the financial loss caused by the death or critical illness of the employee.

The question to answer is, how would the business cope if a key player or fee earner fell under a bus tomorrow? Do you have sufficient resources to take over the present workload and to generate replacement income?

Would an injection of capital into the business at this time be valuable? The same questions are relevant should that player suffer a critical illness and be unable to work, even if only for a limited time or to return with reduced capacity.

Generally, these premiums are deductible against corporation tax providing the key tests are met, the most important being that the relationship is that of an employer and employee. This insurance provides funds that may help to replace the financial loss of the client relationships and associated income to the firm and may even allow the firm to keep trading whilst a suitable replacement is sought.

For those working within limited companies, a relevant life policy may provide very cost- and tax-effective life insurance. It is an alternative way employers can provide death-in-service benefits for employees outside of a registered group life scheme. It is applied for and paid for by the business and written into trust, which pays out a lump sum to trustees for the benefit of the beneficiaries, if employees die or in some cases are diagnosed with a terminal illness. It is a benefit that can make staff feel valued. And it is tax-efficient too – for all parties.

Firms trading as partnerships cannot provide this protection at firm level but the individual partners can provide protection for themselves and their families through a "simple" life insurance contract and an income protection policy.

You may not be able to use key person insurance as a sole practitioner or if you are self-employed; in that case you could rely on income protection insurance, which provides an income if you are ill or injured and cannot work due to an illness.

Succession planning aside, everyone needs to consider what would happen if you become ill or are injured and cannot work. The questions remain – will you still be able to look after yourself and your loved ones financially? How long would your savings last? How you would pay everyday bills such as your mortgage or rent, utilities, food, and other general living costs?

Your personal retirement plan may be relying on a successful exit and succession planning but if you are unable to work, all this could be put at risk.

The state will provide neither an adequate income if you are ill nor sufficient retirement income if you are relying on your state pension.

No one likes paying for insurance; however, it is there for a reason and I have yet to meet anyone who has needed to make a claim who said "I wish I'd had less protection".

Where there is a shareholders' agreement in place, key person protection is often used as the funding vehicle to buy the members' shares should the shareholder die or suffer a critical illness and keep those shares within the firm. This avoids the potential risk that the affected shareholders shares are bequeathed to a family member who has no interest or capability within the business at all. Providing the agreements and cross option agreements are properly drafted, the value of the shareholding will remain exempt from inheritance tax when it is passed to the family and is exchanged for the shares.

Future liabilities

Many solicitors operate on a transactional business model. A prospective purchaser will need to see that there will be a sufficient flow of new enquiries to justify the risk of taking liability for previous transactions. The Solicitors' Indemnity Fund has extended its closure to September 2022, leaving retired and retiring solicitors open to negligence claims perhaps for many years after exit/retirement. Succession plans must be informed by the need for professional indemnity run off cover. Although there is pressure from the Law Society to find alternative solutions, this is set against the backdrop of a general hardening of the PI market. Obtaining adequate run off cover could be the biggest concern of all.

To summarize

If you want to ensure a smooth succession:

- As a firm – have you considered how your agreements and key players fit into the business succession strategy and taken the relevant steps to protect them and the firm for the future?
- As an individual – have you considered how you will maintain your lifestyle when you exit or if you become unable to work through disability? This could be determined by creating your own financial plan. Have you managed to obtain adequate run of cover?

Chapter 8:
Succession planning for sole practitioners

By Shelley Dunstone, principal, Legal Circles

Thinking of retiring?

You've built a legal practice – congratulations on your achievement! It has been successful, providing a good income for you and your family. You have worked hard. But now, retirement age is looming. What will you do when the time comes? Will you be able to sell your practice? Who will look after your clients? Is your practice an asset that can be sold, or will you have to close it down?

Will someone want to buy your practice?

In the past, lawyers who wanted to set up a practice on their own account would look around for a practice to buy. When a senior lawyer announced plans to retire, there would be keen interest from younger lawyers eager to acquire an established practice.

However, times have changed. With new technologies, it is now easier and cheaper than ever before to set up a law firm. You don't even need premises or staff. Many lawyers work from home, visit clients at their homes or businesses, and consult with clients online. Some legal services are delivered entirely via the internet. Voice recognition technology enables a lawyer to work without the expense of a secretary.

Why would someone buy an existing law firm instead of establishing their own?

To make it worth paying money for a law firm, a buyer needs to feel confident that it will put them into a better situation than setting up their own practice from scratch. A buyer might perceive some value in an office that is already set up as a law firm, with desks, computers, and systems such as law firm management software. This would save them some time, effort, and expense. Your location might be near their home or suit their lifestyle in other ways. They might even want to retain some of your staff – secretaries or employed lawyers. But what any buyer is really looking to purchase is an income stream. The question they will ask themselves, and you, is, "How likely is it that clients will stay with this legal practice, and continue to come, after it has changed hands?".

The value of your practice is not determined by the time and effort you have put in to build it. It depends on what income it is likely to generate for a purchaser after you have left.

Options for selling your practice

What options are available to a sole practitioner who wants to sell their practice? Briefly, there are four:

1. **Sell to another firm.** There could be a firm that serves a similar market to yours, and would be keen to grow by acquiring your practice.
2. **Sell to an existing employee.** One of your employed lawyers might be interested in buying your practice and running it as their own.
3. **Employ a lawyer with a view to selling to them in the future.** By employing them, you can help them become familiar with your practice and its clients, so they can gradually transition to ownership.
4. **Sell to an individual newcomer.** There could be a lawyer who is currently employed at another firm, and who is seeking to set up a legal practice on their own account. They might be willing to buy your practice and make it their own.

Each of these options will be discussed in more detail later in this chapter.

What assets can you sell?

What are you really selling when you offer a legal practice for sale? Your assets will fall into the following categories.

- **Tangible assets.** Second-hand desks, chairs, computers, etc. are worth very little. However, the overall set-up of the premises as a law firm could be worth something to a buyer.
- **Intellectual property.** Domain name, website, trademarks, etc.
- **Work in progress (including outlaid disbursements).** These will either be valued at a discount in the sale price or paid out to you when the money is received.
- **Book debts.** These can be included in the purchase price, paid to you when received, or left for you to collect.

- **Client files.** These cannot be sold. Your clients will decide for themselves where to take their business. Some clients might be content for the purchaser to complete their current matters after you have left, but might never return. Others will immediately want to take their work elsewhere. "Files" are synonymous with "work in progress". Their value is the amount of work in progress accrued as at the date of the sale.
- **Goodwill.** The big question is, what is its value?

What is goodwill, and what is it worth?

Goodwill is the amount that a purchaser is willing to pay for a business, over and above the net value of its tangible assets. The value of goodwill is subjective. It depends on who the purchaser is, their particular needs, and what the practice is worth to them.

The amount that a purchaser is willing to pay for goodwill reflects their perception of the benefit to them and the likely future income stream from the practice. What will happen when you leave? Will the current clients stay? Will the practice continue to attract clients? Legal practices are less likely to deliver a reliable income stream than, say, accounting practices. Whereas people need to consult their accountant regularly, legal services tend to be episodic. Purchases of legal services tend to be one-off; sporadic rather than regular. An example of a regular purchaser of legal services is a shopping center that needs leases prepared regularly. What is the nature of your client base – are they occasional or regular purchasers of your legal services?

The marketing of legal services has changed dramatically in recent years. By using targeted internet promotions (advertising or informational content) it might be possible for a newcomer to generate business equally as well as you did, or even better. Therefore, they might not see any value in paying money to you for goodwill.

If your clients have come to the firm because of a close connection with you (the owner), they might not stay after you retire. Often, clients use a law firm because they are friends or long-term acquaintances of the principal, or were referred by a friend or business acquaintance. Probably they also have other lawyer friends, and they might prefer to use their services instead of those of a stranger.

However, if your firm has developed a "brand" that is separate from you, clients might continue to seek out that brand after you have retired. Do clients come to you personally, or do they come to your firm? Does your firm have a website that attracts clients irrespective of their connection with you? Many lawyers take pride in saying, "I never do any marketing. All my work comes through word of mouth." This may sound impressive, but it is not helpful when it comes to selling your practice.

"Local goodwill" is the awareness that there is a legal practice at your location. If your office has a "shop front" presence at street level, and if it has been in its current location for a long time, and if it attracts a lot of passing trade (from people walking along the street), your local goodwill could be worth something. Local goodwill would be of value to someone who wants to take over your office and operate it as their own. They would then receive the benefit of the passing trade. Conversely, a law firm seeking to absorb your practice into its own would only see value in the location of the office if they intend to retain it as a branch of their firm.

If your firm operates in a regional community, and if that community has limited legal services available to it, that could contribute to the value of goodwill. Some regional firms operate in a "captive market". Others compete with city firms, with clients willing to drive to the city to see a lawyer, or to obtain their legal advice through online delivery.

The value of goodwill can be affected by many factors, including:

- The length of time the law firm has been established and has operated under its current name;
- How well-known the firm name is (if it is not the name of the principal);
- The length of time the firm has been at its current location (if it has a street presence);
- The nature of the practice – whether those fields are expanding or declining;
- Future maintainable earnings – will the firm continue to make money when the new owner takes over? Does the firm have continuing retainers with regular clients and referrers? Consider the likelihood of these arrangements being maintained or renewed;
- Whether revenue is increasing, stagnant, or decreasing – a buyer will want to see an upwards trend over several years;
- Whether the owner is willing to stay on for a handover period and introduce the buyer to key clients and referrers;
- Whether the firm has well-trained staff who will be staying on. Often, staff feel connected to the owner and leave when the practice changes hands;

- The quality of information the firm holds about its clients;
- The average size of fee per transaction; and
- Whether the firm is dependent on a small number of clients – if so, it leaves itself vulnerable to their departure.

You should consult a business valuer, but be aware that there will be widely differing views as to the value of goodwill. A valuer will help you set an asking price, but in the end, the value of your practice is what a buyer is willing to pay.

Options available to a seller

Sell to another firm

This is a relatively easy option, but probably the least profitable.

Larger firms might not perceive any goodwill value in your practice, particularly if you will be closing down your office and moving into theirs. They might consider that they are doing you a favor by taking away the burden of your current administrative tasks.

The transaction will be communicated to clients as a "merger" but the term "takeover" would be more apt. You will need to adapt to the new firm's processes and will be subject to management. You will be expected to introduce your clients to other lawyers in the firm, in order to "embed" them into the new organization.

What will happen with your staff? Will the larger firm offer them employment? Will they want to stay? Often, staff who have been used to working with a small firm do not enjoy the larger firm environment. They might not want to come with you, or could leave after a short period of time.

In effect, you are swapping your profits for a regular salary, in a more structured environment with less autonomy. It is up to you to decide whether this is a good deal or not. You will negotiate a process whereby the new firm will pay you for work in progress. You will be expected to stay with the firm for a defined transition period. After that, you might find that you have little job security, and it will indeed be time to retire.

Sell to an existing employee

The advantage of this option is that the clients already know the employee, and are therefore likely to stay (if they have established good relationships with them).

This could also be a disadvantage. Because they already know the clients, there might be nothing to stop your employee setting up their own practice nearby and soliciting your clients. Make sure you include non-compete clauses in your employment contracts.

An employee is arguably in the best possible position to reap the full value of your legal practice, because they will take over your office and the clients are likely to remain with the firm. The real challenge is to find the right person to become your successor, because many lawyers do not want to become business owners.

A gradual transfer of ownership is the best way to ensure maximum value for both vendor and purchaser.

Hire a lawyer with a view to selling to them in the future

Again, the challenge is to find the right person – someone who has the desire and potential to be a business owner. Larger firms pay high salaries, without the burden and responsibility of running a practice. Many lawyers prefer to work in a larger firm because of the social interaction it offers.

It is never easy to predict whether someone will be interested in purchasing your practice, and whether they will carry through with the transaction. Test the waters by having them take on some managerial responsibility. Consider offering them a small equity stake at first. See how they react and how they perform.

During the transition phase, you will need to be mindful of the relationship between you and the new employee. This relationship will be unequal at first, and you should work at balancing it. You will have your own ways of doing things – try to be flexible. Ask your new employee for their ideas and allow them some scope to do things in their own way, or to implement new processes.

Sell to an individual newcomer wanting to commence practice on their own account

This is a quicker and cleaner option than selling to an employee. On a specified date you will hand over ownership in full. However, a buyer will probably want you to stay on for an agreed period of time (perhaps three or six months) to help them settle in and to introduce them to clients and referrers.

You might also be able to negotiate an arrangement whereby you stay on as a consultant, perhaps contributing a percentage of your earnings towards overheads. It could benefit the buyer for you to remain connected to the practice, and you could work in a flexible manner without the burden of administration.

How to maximize your prospects of selling your practice

If there is some lead time before you plan to retire, there are some things you can do to increase the value of your practice and your chances of finding a suitable lawyer to sell it to.

- Work on your firm's branding, to give the firm a life of its own, independent of you. If you don't have a website, get one now. If you have a lot of lead time, consider changing the name of your firm to something other than your name, and work hard on getting that name known. If clients deal with the firm (rather than you as an individual), they will not be quite as sensitive to your departure.
- If you have a website, give it a thorough review and refresh. How effective is it at attracting viewers and converting them into clients? Does it provide valuable information that addresses your clients' typical issues and concerns? Could you even provide services via the internet? Such a revenue stream would be an added attraction for a potential purchaser.
- How well can the practice run without you? Test this when you go away on holidays. How often do staff need to contact you? What questions are they asking you? Could you put in place processes and policies to enable them to act autonomously? Codifying the arrangements you make when you go away could help you set things up for a potential purchaser to come in and run your practice.
- Get your lawyers interested in business ownership. A lot of lawyers are not interested in being business owners. For some people, legal practice is just a job that pays a regular salary. Others might never have thought about owning their own practice. Perhaps you could educate them about the benefits, for example a better income and more autonomy. Show them what the future looks like.
- Have a pipeline of employees, so that when the time comes to retire, you will have a potential successor. In the short-term, it might seem easier to do all the work yourself, but if you never employ anyone you might have to simply close the practice when it's time to retire.
- If you train you are more likely to retain. Improve your training, and have systems for it, to make it easier to replace a lawyer who leaves. Avoid re-inventing the wheel each time a lawyer joins. Set up processes to help them do the work. Learn to delegate well.

- Get your lawyers involved in management activities, and don't leave it too late. Start at a simple level, for example understanding how the trust account works and what expenses the practice incurs. By the time you start thinking about retirement, you want to have staff who feel confident that they could run a law firm. Taking over a practice should not be like becoming a parent for the first time – if you have to learn everything at once it can be very overwhelming.
- Encourage your lawyers to take leadership roles, and to come up with ideas for improvement. Be flexible and take their suggestions seriously. Involve them in business development activities, hiring staff, and firm-wide projects. Talk with them about how to manage and limit risk.
- Finally, evaluate yourself as a role model for your staff. Do you enjoy being a lawyer? Do you like running your own business? Let it show. Be positive and enthusiastic in your interactions at work. A lawyer who sighs and vents, displays their frustration and complains about their clients is unlikely to find a successor amongst their employees.

Conclusion

If you intend to sell your practice one day, you must plan ahead. Build the value of your firm as you practice. If you simply wake up one morning and decide that you have had enough, your options for selling will be very limited. And if you leave it too late, and run out of energy (and clients), there will be nothing left to sell.

Importantly, do not depend on selling your practice to fund your retirement. Over the course of your working life, make sure you set aside some of the income from your successful legal practice, to prepare for life after work.

Chapter 9: Why lawyers and law firms find it difficult to deal with retirement and succession: overcoming the obstacles

By Ronnie Fox, partner, Fox & Partners

I have practiced law in the City of London for over 50 years, starting my career as a corporate and commercial lawyer, and then developing a side-line in employment law, which gradually became my main area of specialization. The formation of the Employment Lawyers Association in 1992 encouraged rapid growth in the number of employment lawyers; that prompted me to focus on the law and practice relating to partnership. I founded and became the first chairman of the Association of Partnership Practitioners in 1998 with a view to securing recognition for partnership law as a separate and distinct area of legal expertise. I founded one law firm in 1989 and another in 2006; both firms continue to bear my name and are going from strength to strength.

I am pleased that my career as a City solicitor is now winding down as I had hoped and planned; my new career as a retirement counsellor is developing. Many lawyers whom I meet love the practice of law and are reluctant to contemplate the prospect of retirement or the implications of succession planning. Having seen many lawyers and law firms struggle with retirement and succession issues, I now set out five principal reasons why lawyers seem to have encountered real difficulty in addressing these topics. Following my description of those reasons are five ideas aimed at helping lawyers to address the issues; I conclude with five suggested solutions to the challenges.

My hope is that consideration of these reasons, the ideas that I outline, and my suggested solutions will prompt lawyers to focus on the issues that are personally relevant, to ask themselves the appropriate questions and to find the answers that are right for them. If you do not ask yourself the correct questions, the likelihood is that nobody will ask you those questions or find the answers for you. Certainly, nobody is in a better position than you are to come up with the way forward right for you.

Five reasons

The first reason lawyers and law firms find it difficult to address the topics of retirement and succession is that there is little or nothing in the education and training of lawyers to equip them to plan for retirement and succession. At the outset of our careers, we are taught about the law, about legal institutions, and about professional ethics. The practical training of solicitors is focused on how to deal with clients and how to resolve their problems. Few lawyers receive any tuition or guidance about career planning. I have advised a number of mature lawyers who were surprised and shocked to hear from a senior or managing partner that their withdrawal was being sought to make equity available to younger partners.

The second is that the essence of being a professional is that clients' interests take precedence over one's own personal interests. The pressures of professional life are often so great that many lawyers neglect the need to plan their own careers or to manage the medium- and long-term financial requirements of themselves, their dependents, their practice, and their professional colleagues. Indeed, many lawyers and law firms do not even treat the management of their own firms as "real" work. It is often regarded as a distraction to take time to plan how to manage, to progress, or to wind down one's own professional life or to work out how to handle the sharing of clients' affairs with colleagues and ultimately the transfer of client relationships to colleagues. A crucial indicator is the way in which some lawyers in a firm talk about "my" clients, not about "our" clients. The security of partners in a law firm is often intimately connected to the value of their personal book of business, the amount of professional work that individual partners are able to generate, and the size of their own teams. That security is threatened by talk of retirement and succession. The concept of voluntarily helping clients and contacts build relationships with colleagues with a view to reinforcing connections with the firm as a whole – and ultimately replacing your own relationships – is challenging.

Thirdly, one way in which we are all indisputably equal is that each of us has only 24 hours in a day. Nearly every lawyer whom I have ever met has more to do than time in which to do it. Even if a lawyer or a law firm manager knows deep down that retirement and succession are difficult and complex topics that will have to be addressed one day, there is a natural and understandable tendency to put such matters on the back burner, to assure oneself that, "I will get around to it". Sooner or later, clients, colleagues, and family are bound to become impatient if you simply refuse to talk about how you intend to adjust for the passing of the years, to accommodate the desire of younger partners for client relationships and an increasing share of profits, or to adjust to the changing extent of your role at home. That illustrates the futility and foolishness of procrastinating, of putting off the decisions and plans that need to be addressed.

The fourth issue is the current pace of change in the legal profession. Older lawyers tend to find it more difficult to adapt to change. Keeping up-to-date with legal and regulatory developments is a significant burden. Technology now has a huge impact on the practice of law. We are increasingly dependent on computers and smartphones, on webinars, virtual meetings, and email chains. The security and resilience of internet connections has become a major concern. Algorithms and artificial intelligence are generating decisions of increasing significance. I recently heard a brilliant lawyer in his 50s refuse to engage with any form of social media or to come to terms with the role of social media in the generation of new business. The pandemic has compelled lawyers to tackle new ways of remote working and to experiment with hybrid working models; senior lawyers are often reluctant to give up positions that enable them to control the speed at which they engage with change.

The fifth and most serious reason why both individual lawyers and law firms are so uncomfortable planning for retirement and succession is because by doing so one is forced to confront challenges such as aging, the decline in mental powers that is frequently associated with increasing age, the potential need for expensive healthcare, and ultimately one's own mortality. The plain facts are that we change as we age, many of us will face health issues, and all of us are going to die.

Five ideas

There can be no universally successful strategies for organizing retirement and succession within law firms. Experience has taught me that a few elements almost always contribute to a successful outcome. Here are five ideas that I offer with a view to assisting lawyers and law firms to address challenges associated with retirement and succession.

First, recognize that seeking to plan ahead is a mature and sensible thing to do. Are you the sort of person or business manager who drifts though life letting things happen to you and your business or do you set yourself targets, objectives, and milestones – and then work to achieve them? Clients and colleagues become upset by unanticipated developments; they tend to be reassured by a clear plan. The most important aspect of a first meeting with a new client is agreement on the way forward and the next steps.

Second, think about how you want to be remembered. Is your legacy going to be files in a mess, clients who are unhappy because they do not know who will look after them when you are less active, and younger colleagues who are resentful because you have not made efforts to share with them your relationships and your experiences? The more crucial you believe you are to the continuing success of your practice, the more important it becomes to share with your colleagues the benefit of your experience. It is wonderful to hear former colleagues with whom you worked years ago tell you that when they encounter a problem, they still think about how you would have dealt with it.

Third, imagine the kudos that will attach to your name and the prestige you will earn for your firm and family if you focus in good time on making a success out of succession for the business, for colleagues, for clients, and for yourself. I remember a group of partners in one law firm who became convinced that their new senior partner was insufficiently sensitive to the differences between (1) a listed trading company where major decisions regarding the future of the business are made by a small board of directors, and (2) a professional partnership where those managing the practice need to carry the hearts and minds of partners with them. The name, reputation, and culture of that firm, developed over many years, disappeared within a few weeks following a so-called "merger".

Fourth, accept that people change as they age and adjust accordingly. It is futile to pretend that mental and physical abilities do not change with age or that an older partner who has played a major role in establishing the financial stability of a practice should therefore always be entitled to receive more money than a younger partner. Older people have different strengths and weaknesses. In my view, an important reason why many US-based law firms have been very successful in London is that they are often better at understanding and exploiting the experience and achievements of some of their older partners to the advantage both of those lawyers and of the firm as a whole. By contrast, some highly regarded and long-established London-based law firms have fixed retirement ages stipulated in their partnership agreements or consider that they can only accommodate the ambitions of younger partners by forcing the expulsion of partners in their fifties.

Finally, consider yourself extremely fortunate if you have reached maturity in your legal career and continue to enjoy the work that you do. Sadly, some lawyers only discover that they dislike the practice of law at a relatively late stage in their careers, i.e. after they have acquired a mortgage, family responsibilities, and a variety of financial liabilities. Even if you love your work as a lawyer, bear in mind that no extra points or credits are awarded to those who die at their desk. Most people are familiar with the observation that as the end of life approaches, nobody ever wishes that they had recorded more chargeable hours; however, that is exactly the point in life when many people find themselves wishing that they had spent more time with family and friends, more time making life easier for their successors, and more time devoted to community and charitable projects.

My hope is that partners and managers in law firms will regard these ideas as helpful and relevant and that will assist them to devise bespoke strategies for themselves and their firms.

Five solutions

Let us be positive. Here are five proven ways of smoothing the path to retirement and succession.

1. **Planning** for the future

It has never been more difficult for businesses to plan for the future. The challenges range from climate change to oppressive over-regulation, from diversity quotas to information technology, from political change to pandemics. Many of today's largest and most successful businesses did not exist a generation ago. Other companies that just a few years ago were world leaders in their sector have virtually disappeared. Kodak dominated the market for photographic film in the 20th century; the company pioneered digital photography but did not foresee that one consequence would be an almost complete collapse in the demand for traditional film. As a result, Kodak filed for chapter 11 bankruptcy in 2012. No matter how difficult it may be, the importance of planning remains. A law firm that intends to endure should plan to facilitate the recruitment, training, and promotion of the next generation of leaders whilst providing financial and structural inducements for the older generation not only to support transition but also to contemplate individual paths leading to retirement.

2. Choosing the right **People**

Statistics published by the Solicitors Regulation Authority[1] indicate that the number of sole practitioners operating legal practices in England and Wales fell from 3,612 in September 2011 to 1,921 in September 2021, a drop of almost 47 percent in ten years. (By way of contrast, during the same period the total number of solicitors' firms fell from 11,009 to 9,943, a drop of less than ten percent.) Sole practitioners now only account for a fifth of practitioners overall, compared to one in three a decade ago. Perhaps one significant explanation is the increasingly broad range of skills now required to run a successful law firm. The key to long-term management success is identifying the strengths of each member of the firm and persuading individuals to play to their strengths. That involves recruiting, developing and promoting the right mixture of finders, minders, and grinders, i.e. those who bring in clients, those who look after clients, and those who do the legal work. To survive retirements and ensure succession, law firms need access to a blend of legal and business abilities. Few individuals have all the required skills. I know one lawyer who introduced many clients in a specific industry to his firm and built a reputation for his firm as a leading firm of solicitors in that industry; he always admitted to his partners that he was not much of a technical lawyer and he ensured that specific legal advice was given to clients by his colleagues. I know an able and experienced litigation partner in a law firm who does not appreciate the difference between revenue and profit; he believes that the effect of reducing charge-out rates by five percent is to reduce profits by five percent. I have seen several firms forced into a merger – and the inevitable dilution of the specific ethos and culture developed over the years – when the principals started searching for an exit but realized too late in the day that their team lacked the right blend of technical, managerial, and business skills.

3. Remembering that the survival of every law firm depends on **Profit**

In a capitalist society, only firms that are consistently profitable can survive and prosper. Together the guides to law firms, the specialist legal press, the requirements for limited companies and limited liability partnerships to publish accounts, and the surveys conducted by accountants and legal head-hunters mean that more is now known than ever before about the profitability of different law firms. Relatively unprofitable firms are unlikely to attract and retain the right partners and staff; any efforts those firms may make with a view to facilitating succession will probably be wasted.

4. Creating a gradual **Path** to retirement

Firms need either to include in their partnership agreements or less formally to adopt policies to encourage partners to make financial provision for their retirement (which may take the form of introductions to a trusted financial adviser, a clearly expressed expectation that partners will each year set aside a certain percentage of their income to provide for their retirement, a timetable offering a gradual path towards partner retirement, and a soft landing at the point of retirement). Managing partner expectations in this way will reduce the risk of unhappiness and damaging disputes.

Designing the path needs to take account of the psychological impact of retirement of the old guard (and also of the promotion of their successors). To a great extent our identity is defined by what we do. Those who have presented themselves for many years as a lawyer and a partner in a law firm may fear losing a significant part of their identity on the way to retirement. A positive approach is to regard retirement as a new career – as one door closes, a new one opens. Successful law firms often provide help during this process, for example, by facilitating a gradual transition from providing full-time frontline legal advice, via a part-time internal consulting role supporting, coaching and mentoring the next generation of partners whilst allowing time for the development of new interests and relationships, prior to a complete withdrawal from legal practice. I am haunted by the memory of a successful partner who worked flat-out until the day he retired completely at the age of 70, apparently in good health; he died just six weeks later.

5. Helping colleagues to **Progress** as retiring partners wind down

Major obstacles to succession in law firms are remuneration and management structures which allow – or even encourage – partners to work in silos. Ideally, partners should receive incentives for training and developing younger colleagues. It is almost invariably in the short-term financial interests of clients and the long-term interests of law firms that partners work on every project with an associate. Ideally every associate should be mentored by a partner responsible for ensuring that the associate receives an appropriate mixture of legal work, business training, and practice development opportunities. The partner will also have an opportunity of learning from the associate. The two-way mentoring process will help associates to grow and develop in a way that will generate their own confidence in themselves and inspire confidence in those clients whom they serve together with, and ultimately in succession to, retiring partners.

Experienced professionals have honed their management and communication styles. Their successors will need to adapt and learn to manage people, to generate client relationships, and to share their experiences in different ways that will involve many ways of communicating. Traditionally the academic training of solicitors has included little or nothing about psychology, business, or marketing. Typically, partners winding down to retirement will have accumulated many years of experience and knowledge of basic human behavior, of maintaining cashflow by limiting lock-up and exercising credit control, and of understanding why potential clients choose to instruct one firm rather than another. There are numerous ways in which law firms can facilitate succession by enabling and encouraging retiring partners to share their experience and knowledge with the next generation of partners. The dice are heavily loaded in favor of the firms that do so.

References

1. www.sra.org.uk/sra/how-we-work/reports/statistics/regulated-community-statistics/data/solicitor_firms/

About Globe Law and Business

Globe Law and Business was established in 2005. From the very beginning, we set out to create law books which are sufficiently high level to be of real use to the experienced professional, yet still accessible and easy to navigate. Most of our authors are drawn from Magic Circle and other top commercial firms, both in the UK and internationally.

Our titles are carefully produced, with the utmost attention paid to editorial, design and production processes. We hope this results in high-quality publications that are easy to read, and a pleasure to own. Our titles are also available as ebooks, which are compatible with most desktop, laptop and tablet devices. In 2018 we expanded our portfolio to include journals and Special Reports, available both digitally and in hard copy format, and produced to the same high standards as our books.

In the spring of 2021, we were very pleased to announce the start of a new chapter for Globe Law and Business following the acquisition of law books under the imprint Ark Publishing. We are very much looking forward to working with our new Ark authors, many of whom are well known to us, to further developing the law firm management list, and to welcoming our new Ark customers.

We'd very much like to hear from you with your thoughts and ideas for improving what we offer. Please do feel free to email me at sian@globelawandbusiness.com with your views.

Sian O'Neill
Managing director
Globe Law and Business
www.globelawandbusiness.com

www.ingramcontent.com/pod-product-compliance
Ingram Content Group UK Ltd.
Pitfield, Milton Keynes, MK11 3LW, UK
UKHW021848150926
8657IPUK00005B/140

9 781787 4283